Quorum Systems

with Applications to Storage and Consensus

Synthesis Lectures on Distributed Computing Theory

Editor
Nancy Lynch, ***Massachusetts Institute of Technology***

Synthesis Lectures on Distributed Computing Theory is edited by Nancy Lynch of the Massachusetts Institute of Technology. The series will publish 50- to 150 page publications on topics pertaining to distributed computing theory. The scope will largely follow the purview of premier information and computer science conferences, such as ACM PODC, DISC, SPAA, OPODIS, CONCUR, DialM-POMC, ICDCS, SODA, Sirocco, SSS, and related conferences. Potential topics include, but not are limited to: distributed algorithms and lower bounds, algorithm design methods, formal modeling and verification of distributed algorithms, and concurrent data structures.

Quorum Systems with Applications to Storage and Consensus
Marko Vukolić
2012

Link Reversal Algorithms
Jennifer L. Welch and Jennifer E. Walter
2011

Cooperative Task-Oriented Computing: Algorithms and Complexity
Chryssis Georgiou and Alexander A. Shvartsman
2011

New Models for Population Protocols
Othon Michail, Ioannis Chatzigiannakis, and Paul G. Spirakis
2011

The Theory of Timed I/O Automata, Second Edition
Dilsun K. Kaynar, Nancy Lynch, Roberto Segala, and Frits Vaandrager
2010

Principles of Transactional Memory
Rachid Guerraoui and Michal Kapalka
2010

Fault-tolerant Agreement in Synchronous Message-passing Systems
Michel Raynal
2010

Communication and Agreement Abstractions for Fault-Tolerant Asynchronous Distributed Systems
Michel Raynal
2010

The Mobile Agent Rendezvous Problem in the Ring
Evangelos Kranakis, Danny Krizanc, and Euripides Markou
2010

Quorum Systems with Applications to Storage and Consensus

Marko Vukoli´c

ISBN:978-3-031-00879-5 paperback
ISBN:978-3-031-02007-0 ebook

DOI 10.1007/978-3-031-02007-0

A Publication in the Springer series
SYNTHESIS LECTURES ON DISTRIBUTED COMPUTING THEORY

Lecture #9
Series Editor: Nancy Lynch, *Massachusetts Institute of Technology*
Series ISSN
Synthesis Lectures on Distributed Computing Theory
Print 2155-1626 Electronic 2155-1634

Quorum Systems

with Applications to Storage and Consensus

Marko Vukolić
Eurécom

SYNTHESIS LECTURES ON DISTRIBUTED COMPUTING THEORY #9

ABSTRACT

A quorum system is a collection of subsets of nodes, called quorums, with the property that each pair of quorums have a non-empty intersection. Quorum systems are the key mathematical abstraction for ensuring consistency in fault-tolerant and highly available distributed computing.

Critical for many applications since the early days of distributed computing, quorum systems have evolved from simple majorities of a set of processes to complex hierarchical collections of sets, tailored for general adversarial structures. The initial non-empty intersection property has been refined many times to account for, e.g., stronger (Byzantine) adversarial model, latency considerations or better availability. This monograph is an overview of the evolution and refinement of quorum systems, with emphasis on their role in two fundamental applications: distributed read/write storage and consensus.

KEYWORDS

consensus, intersection, quorums, replication, storage

To the eternal memory of my beloved mother Mirjana and my father Miloš

Contents

Preface xiii

Acknowledgments xv

1 Introduction 1

1.1 Origins 1
1.2 Relevance 2
1.3 Scope of the Monograph 2
1.4 Organization of the Monograph 3

2 Preliminaries 5

2.1 Processes and Communication Models 5
2.2 Process failures 6
2.3 Timing Assumptions 8
2.4 Read/Write Storage 9
2.5 Consensus 12
2.6 Pseudocode Conventions 13

3 Classical Quorum Systems 15

3.1 Basics 15
3.2 Examples 16
3.3 Measures 18
3.3.1 Load 18
3.3.2 Availability 21
3.3.3 Failure Probability 22
3.3.4 Comparison 23
3.4 Bibliographic Notes 23

4 Classical Quorum-Based Emulations 25

4.1 Storage Emulation 25
4.1.1 The setup 26
4.1.2 The algorithm 26

4.1.3 Correctness Arguments 28
4.2 Consensus emulation 31
4.2.1 Synod Termination 31
4.2.2 Quorum-based SynodOFC 32
4.3 Dynamic Storage Emulation 36
4.3.1 The *Recon* component 38
4.3.2 The *RWC* component 40
4.3.3 The *Joiner* component 47
4.4 Bibliographic Notes 47

5 Byzantine Quorum Systems 51
5.1 Dissemination Quorum Systems 52
5.1.1 Basics 52
5.1.2 Storage emulation 56
5.1.3 Consensus emulation 59
5.2 Masking Quorum Systems 67
5.2.1 Basics 68
5.2.2 Storage emulation 72
5.3 Opaque Quorum Systems 75
5.3.1 Basics 75
5.3.2 Storage emulation 77
5.4 Bibliographic Notes 77

6 Latency-efficient Quorum Systems 81
6.1 Introduction 81
6.2 Refined Quorum Systems 82
6.2.1 Basics 82
6.2.2 Intuition 84
6.2.3 Examples 84
6.3 Emulations 91
6.3.1 Fast Consensus 91
6.3.2 Fast Byzantine Storage 98
6.4 Bibliographic notes 107

7 Probabilistic Quorum Systems 109
7.1 Introduction 109
7.2 ϵ-Intersecting Quorum Systems 110

7.3 (b, ϵ)-dissemination quorum systems ... 113
7.4 Bibliographic Notes ... 115

Bibliography ... **117**

Author's Biography ... **125**

Index ... **127**

Preface

Why a book on quorum systems? Quorum systems are seemingly very simple. After all, quorum systems are simple collections of pairwise intersecting sets. Whereas understanding mathematical definition of a quorum system might seem straightforward, understanding distributed computing, on the other hand, is not an easy task. Consequently, understanding different quorum systems in distributed computing becomes more involved. Moreover, the initial mathematical definition of quorums has evolved in many ways throughout the history of using quorums in distributed computing, effectively blurring the clarity of the original definition.

Today, many notions of quorums systems in distributed computing exist. These include probabilistic, dynamic, signed, timed, Byzantine, fast, refined, and many more. Each of the mentioned quorum systems has been used in the literature to facilitate a solution to some distributed computing problems including most fundamental ones, like mutual exclusion, registers, consensus and state machine replication to name a few. Different variants of quorum systems have been used to solve or implement more efficiently these abstractions under widely different assumptions that involve asynchrony, different types of process failures, churn, etc. Indeed, quorum systems are fundamental to distributed computing and have been a basic abstraction in building countless distributed systems.

However, despite the wealth of research dedicated, either implicitly or explicitly, to using different notions of quorums in distributed computing, this research lacks structure that would help a novice student answer few basic questions, such as: Why are new quorum systems invented? What are the main differences among different quorum notions? Which quorum system should I use to solve a specific problem under given assumptions? Which quorums should I use to optimize a distributed system?

This monograph. This monograph precisely aims at filling this structural gap in quorum systems literature and answering, at least to some extent, some of the questions stated above. The focal distributed computing abstractions in this monograph are registers (also called read/write storage) and consensus (or, more generally, replication). We believe these abstractions to be at the same time fundamental and practically relevant. At the same time, read/write storage and consensus are very suitable for presenting similarities and differences among different quorum notions. While many books that treat the notions of read/write storage and consensus exists our angle is obviously emphasizing the quorum systems perspective.

Readership. This monograph has been written primarily for the people who are not experts in the topics presented. This includes graduate students and senior-level Master students in computer science and computer engineering who nurture interest in the foundations of distributed computing.

Besides, some later chapters can also be useful to experts in fault-tolerant distributed computing who are interested in quickly grasping the advanced and more recent quorum systems concepts. Prerequisites for this monograph include basic undergraduate courses on algorithms. Previous knowledge of distributed systems is helpful but is not necessary.

Marko Vukolić
February 2012

Acknowledgments

I am grateful to Nancy Lynch for providing me with an opportunity to write this monograph and Rachid Guerraoui for suggesting me to write the monograph in the first place. I am also very grateful to Christian Cachin for valuable comments on the earlier drafts of the monograph. Many thanks go to the executive editor, Diane Cerra, for her patience and for always being positive.

Above all, I am deeply grateful to my beloved late parents—my mother Mirjana and my father Miloš—for everything they taught me, for their endless love and for every inspiring moment I spent with them.

Marko Vukolić
February 2012

CHAPTER 1

Introduction

1.1 ORIGINS

The very etymology of the word *quorum* ('of whom', Latin genitive plural of *qui*, who) is an indication of its importance, as it denotes a selected group. Quorums have been used for centuries in law and legislative terminology, to denote the number of 'officers or members of a body that when duly assembled is legally competent to transact business'.[1] A historical example of such a 'business' is the process of *voting*. A typical number of members of a quorum in a the voting process is usually a majority. Intuitively, requiring majorities to reach decisions in a voting process is critical in preventing inconsistencies and partitioning in a legislative process, which are clearly undesirable. However, even in law, quorums can have sizes different than ordinary majorities, such as two-thirds majorities, in the case of constitutional changes. Sometimes, a quorum can contain even less than a majority, for example in cases where the decisions taken are not so critical.

Quorums have revealed vital to distributed computing ever since its early days, dating back to the late 1970s. In distributed computing, quorums come in groups, forming *quorum systems*. Given a set of nodes, typically servers, the basic definition stipulates a quorum system as a collections of subsets of nodes, called quorums, every two of which intersect. A set of majorities is both a fundamental and obvious example of a quorum system.

The historical use of quorums has arguably inspired their use in computer science. Namely, the *raison d'être* of quorum systems in distributed computing is to guarantee *consistency*. Consider, for example, a read/write distributed storage system consisting of three processes. Intuitively, writing a value in any two processes (a majority) guarantees that a subsequent read from any two processes will return a consistent value. Clearly, the key property of quorum systems to guaranteeing consistency is that of non-empty pairwise intersections. In this scheme, the intersection property guarantees that the reader will obtain the latest value. This property is critical in preserving consistency in the presence of potential network partitions.

Quorum systems research had to wait for a solution to fundamental problems of clock synchronization and ordering of (potentially conflicting) events in a distributed system [Lamport, 1978a]. Then the research focus quickly shifted to ensuring consistency in a replicated distributed system and quorum systems were born. Early works that have marked the dawn of quorum systems research [Lamport, 1978b, Thomas, 1979] have evolved around majorities. [Lamport, 1978b] deals with consistency in the context of fault-tolerant state machine replication in synchronous systems, referring to quorums as "amoebas", arguing that a useful "amoeba" should be "large enough", i.e.,

[1] `http://www.merriam-webster.com/dictionary/quorum.`

contain a majority (of processes). [Thomas, 1979] proposed a majority approach to solving consensus to maintain concurrency control over multiple copies of a replicated database. Thomas used a majority voting scheme in which database copies vote on the acceptability of update requests. To write data to the database, the writer would timestamp [Lamport, 1978a] the data and write it to a majority of servers. Then, to read the data, the reader would contact a (possibly different) majority, and return the data having the highest timestamp.

Shortly after these early works, quorum systems were defined in a more general context, refining the concept of majorities to allow arbitrary quorum sizes while maintaining the requirement for non-empty pair-wise quorum intersections. Notably, [Gifford, 1979] introduced a weighted voted scheme and was also the first to refine the concept of majority-based quorums by separating the notions of read and write quorums. In this fundamental refinement, the quorum intersection property is relaxed so as not to require all quorums to intersect. Namely, [Gifford, 1979] separated quorums into two classes: *read* and *write* quorums, and requires only quorums belonging to different classes to intersect.

Other quorum system refinements followed, and today, more than three decades later, new refinements still emerge. The main goal of this monograph is to explain fundamental aspects of quorum systems with a special attention on the refinements of a basic non-empty intersection property, witnessed in modern quorum systems.

1.2 RELEVANCE

As mentioned earlier, consistency is the critical aspect of quorum systems. The other important aspect of quorums, namely that they are (typically strict) subsets of a set of processes, relates to the goals of higher availability [Naor and Wool, 1998], better load balancing [Holzman et al., 1997] and fault-tolerance [Barbara and Garcia-Molina, 1986] in distributed systems. The key idea here is that a client accessing a (replicated) service does not necessarily need to communicate with all the nodes, but only with the nodes belonging to some quorum, which is itself often a strict subset of nodes. This leads to relaxation of the load on nodes that reside outside of a quorum and/or enables tolerance of their failures, resulting in higher availability.

In this context, quorum systems have been used to implement a wide variety of distributed objects and services. Typical examples include replicated databases [Gifford, 1979, Herlihy, 1986, Thomas, 1979], mutual exclusion [Agrawal and El Abbadi, 1989, Maekawa, 1985], read/write storage [Attiya et al., 1995, Malkhi and Reiter, 1998a] and group communication [Amir et al., 1995, Birman and Renesse, 1994], to name only a very few.

1.3 SCOPE OF THE MONOGRAPH

A comprehensive survey of all the protocols and techniques that rely on the notion of quorums is beyond the scope of this monograph due to the sheer number of quorum-based distributed algorithms. On the other hand, the goal of this monograph is to overview the evolution of quorum systems in distributed computing literature, with particular emphasis on refinements of the original quorum notion. Specifically, our goal is to overview how the simple non-empty intersection property has evolved in time and to attempt to explain different quorum access methods of a given quorum system, in terms of different model assumptions and design goals.

However, the story of quorum systems would be incomplete without exemplifying at least some applications that rely upon them. In this monograph we follow the evolution of quorum systems through two fundamental distributed applications: distributed storage and consensus. Besides their fundamental importance, these applications were arguably the main drivers of the quorum system evolution and hence serve as good examples of the subtle differences among various quorum notions.

Additionally, and for completeness, we overview some of the main quorum systems concepts and measures such as load and availability.

1.4 ORGANIZATION OF THE MONOGRAPH

The rest of this monograph is organized as follows. Chapter 2 contains mathematical preliminaries and definitions of basic distributed computing abstractions we refer to later in the monograph.

Chapter 3 describes classical quorum systems as well as few fundamental measures (e.g., load, availability) typically used to evaluate quorum systems.

Chapter 4 shows how to use classical quorums in the context of read/write storage and consensus, first in a context of a static membership, and then within a dynamic quorum membership context.

We depart from the crash failure model in Chapter 5 where we present three families of Byzantine quorum systems: dissemination, masking and opaque quorum systems.

Chapter 6 discusses quorum systems specifically tailored to be enable latency-efficient distributed storage and consensus implementations. In particular, it presents refined quorum systems, which further refine classical and Byzantine quorum systems, with the goal of designing strongly consistent distributed protocols with optimal latency.

Finally, Chapter 7 briefly describes probabilistic quorum systems (PQS) that probabilistically relax the intersection property of classical quorum systems to provide better availability.

Storage and consensus algorithms that exemplify the use of different quorum systems are included throughout the presentation.

The content of this monograph is based on the work previously published in [Vukolić, 2010].

CHAPTER 2

Preliminaries

This chapter introduces preliminary distributed computing definitions, namely: process communication models, process failure models, timing assumptions, as well as specifications of problems we are interested in: read/write storage and consensus. For a more complete introduction to distributed computing, we refer the reader to standard textbooks [Attiya and Welch, 1998, Cachin et al., 2011, Lynch, 1996].

2.1 PROCESSES AND COMMUNICATION MODELS

Processes. We model the behavior of a computer program as a *process*. A distributed system consists of a set of such processes, denoted by S, each process running a particular algorithm. Processes are possibly (but not necessarily) running on a different hardware. In principle, we consider systems with the fixed number of processes, denoted by n. Elements of S are distinguished by process identifiers and denoted by $S = \{s_1, s_2, \ldots, s_n\}$.

Remark 2.1 Exceptionally, in Chapter 4.3 we also deal with systems with *dynamic process membership*, where the number of processes is unbounded and where processes can join and leave the system.

A process is a state machine (or an I/O automaton [Lynch and Tuttle, 1989]) whose states are divided into variables, and that has a set of discrete actions, which classify as internal and external. External actions might be input actions (e.g., when a process receives a message) or output actions (e.g., when a process sends a message). Internal and external actions may change the state of a process. Each process is sequential in a sense that it deterministically run their algorithm instructions step by step. However, different processes execute their algorithms concurrently: hence, their steps can interleave.

When processes run the distributed algorithm, they generate *executions*. An execution is a (possibly infinite) sequence of alternating global system states st_j and individual process actions π_j, starting with an initial state denoted by $initState$, or st_0. For example, an execution is $st_0, \pi_1, st_1, \pi_2, st_2, \ldots$; where each triple (st_i, π_i, st_{i+1}) denotes a *step*, and its associated state transition. A *partial execution* is a finite prefix of some execution. A (partial) execution ex *extends* some partial execution ex' if ex' is a prefix of ex.

In order to effectively run a distributed algorithm, processes need to communicate from time to time. In this manuscript, we consider two basic communication models: the message-passing model and the shared memory model.

Message-passing model. In this communication model, processes communicate by sending and receiving messages. In the message-passing model, we assume that processes are fully interconnected by bidirectional point-to-point channels, i.e., each pair of processes is connected by a bidirectional point-to-point channel.

Processes exchange message using $send$ (an output action) and $receive$ (an input action) events which are assumed to be atomic. However, since we are dealing with point-to-point channel multicasts and broadcasts are not atomic. For example, "$send$ to all" algorithm instruction is not atomic.

Shared memory model. In this communication model, processes communicate by executing *operation* on *shared objects*, which are, like processes, modeled as automatons. A shared object exports several operations, depending on its specification. To execute operation op on shared object O, process s *invokes* op on O which we denote by $inv_s(O, op)$ (via an output action for s, which is in turn an input action for O). Then, s receives a *response* $resp_s(O, v)$ (via an output action of O, which is in turn an input action for s), where v is the value returned by an operation. We refer to the invocation/response pair as to *operation execution*, denoted by $O.op_s \rightarrow v$.

An operation execution can be *complete*, if an invocation event is followed by a response. Otherwise, an operation execution is called *pending*. For simplicity, with slight abuse of language, we sometimes simply write "operation" when we should be referring to operation execution.

2.2 PROCESS FAILURES

We consider fault-prone distributed systems in which processes and shared objects might be faulty. We confine our exposition to two basic fault models: crash faults and Byzantine faults. In short, a faulty process might deviate (i.e., be Byzantine) or stop (i.e., crash) the execution of the algorithm assigned to it.

Definition 2.2 Benign and correct processes If a process (or a shared object) does not deviate from the algorithm assign to it (in execution ex), it is called *benign* (in ex). Moreover, if a benign process does not stop executing the algorithm assigned to it, it is called *correct* (in ex).

Definition 2.3 Crash faults A benign process (resp., shared object) is said to be *crash* faulty, if it stops executing its algorithm prematurely (resp., if it does not respond to an operation). After the process (object) crashes, it does not perform any additional step.

Definition 2.4 Byzantine faults A process that is not benign is called *Byzantine*.

By Definitions 2.2 and 2.4, a Byzantine [Lamport et al., 1982b] process (sometimes also called arbitrary faulty process [Jayanti et al., 1998]) might deviate from the algorithm automaton assigned to it in a way different than simply crashing.

In this monograph we distinguish two models that define the possible behavior of Byzantine processes and shared objects:

1. In the first model, called *unauthenticated*, a Byzantine process s_B can perform arbitrary actions: (a) s_B can send arbitrary messages (in the message-passing model) or invoke arbitrary operations with arbitrary operation parameters on shared objects (in the shared memory model); and (b) s_B can change its state in an arbitrary manner. Similarly, a Byzantine shared object might return an arbitrary response to an operation. Notice that, in the message passing model, we assume that channels are *secure*, i.e., that a Byzantine process s_B cannot send or remove any message from the point-to-point channel that links two benign processes.

2. The second model, called *authenticated*, is strictly stronger than the unauthenticated model. Namely, in the authenticated model, we assume that every process can produce cryptographic digital signatures. The functionality of the digital signature scheme provides two operations: σ for signing and V for signature verification. The invocation of σ takes a process ID, say s_i, and a bit string m as parameters and returns a bit string sig, called a *signature*. The verification operation V takes a process ID s_i, and two bit strings m and sig as parameters and returns a boolean. The verification function has the property that $V(s_i, m, sig)$ invoked by a benign process evaluates to $true$ if and only if process s_i executed $\sigma(s_i, m)$ in some previous step. Furthermore, no process (including Byzantine ones) other than s_i may invoke $\sigma(s_i, m)$ (we say signatures are *unforgeable*); hence, alternatively, we also write $\sigma(s_i, m)$ as $\sigma_{s_i}(m)$. In the following, we refer to a pair $(m, \sigma_{s_i}(m))$ as $m_{\sigma_{s_i}}$ (we say that m is an *authenticated* or *digitally signed* message or value, depending on the context of m). Moreover, if a benign process can evaluate $V(s_i, m, sig)$ to $true$ (i.e., if $sig = \sigma_{s_i}(m)$), we say that a pair (m, sig) contains a *valid* signature (or, alternatively, that (m, sig) is *valid*).

Auxiliary definitions. To conveniently capture the fault state across the entire system we introduce the notion of *fault configurations*.

Definition 2.5 Fault Configuration A fault configuration is a vector $\mathbf{c} \in \{0, 1\}^n$ such that $c_i = 1$ if and only if the process s_i has failed.

Notation 2.6 Given a set of processes S, and an execution ex we denote the set of correct processes in S by $alive(ex, S)$, and the set of faulty process in S by $faulty(ex, S)$. When ex is understood, we simply write $alive(S)$, resp., $faulty(S)$.

Definition 2.7 Availability A set of processes $Q \subseteq S$ is *available* (in some execution ex) if $Q \in alive(S)$.

The probabilistic fault model. For the sake of evaluating different quorum systems we will use the simple probabilistic fault model, that applies to both crash and Byzantine faults. In practice, the fault model can often depart from the probabilistic one, yet the probabilistic fault model provides us with the simple and understandable tool for evaluating different quorum system measures and allows us to compare the quality of different quorum systems.

Definition 2.8 Probabilistic fault model In the *probabilistic fault model*, we assume that each process s_i in a set of processes S fails independently with probability p_i. In the special case, when $p_i = p$ for every process s_i, we talk about *uniform* probabilistic fault model.

2.3 TIMING ASSUMPTIONS

Communication among processes, be it in the message-passing or shared memory model, can be *synchronous* or *asynchronous*. In both timing models, we assume: (a) that processes take internal steps of their algorithms in negligible time; and (b) a global clock. In the asynchronous model, the notion of global clock is external to the system: processes and shared objects do not have access to the global clock in the asynchronous model.

Synchronous model. In the synchronous model, we assume that all communication takes a finite amount of time, δ, known to processes. In particular, in the message-passing model, we assume that a message sent between two correct processes at time t is received by $t + \delta$. Similarly, a correct shared object invoked by a correct process at time t, must respond by $t + \delta$.

Asynchronous model. In the asynchronous model there are no bounds on message propagation delays and the time for response of shared objects. However, we assume *reliable* channels: a message sent between two correct processes (resp., a correct shared object invoked by a correct process) is eventually received (resp., eventually responds).

Synchronous periods in the asynchronous model. We say that an asynchronous message-passing system is *synchronous* (during time interval $[t, t']$) if, for every two correct processes s_1 and s_2, the propagation delay of every message sent by s_1 to s_2 (during time interval $[t, t']$) is at most one time unit Δ, where Δ is known to all correct processes. Similarly, we say that a set of processes S is synchronous if the above holds for every two correct processes $s_1, s_2 \in S$. Analogously, we make use of the notion of synchronous periods in the asynchronous shared memory model.

Eventually synchronous model. An asynchronous system is called *eventually synchronous* [Dwork et al., 1988] if it is synchronous after some time GST (global stabilization time). GST is not known to processes/shared objects.

Time complexity in the asynchronous model. In this monograph we rely on the definition of *time complexity* of an asynchronous algorithm adapted from [Peterson and Fischer, 1977].

To define time complexity, we use the notion of *propagation delay*. The *propagation delay* of message m is the difference between the time receiver s_j receives m and the time sender s_i sends m (according to the global clock).

Definition 2.9 Time complexity The (worst-case) *time complexity* (or *latency*) of an asynchronous algorithm is the worst-case number of time units over all possible executions from the start to the completion of the algorithm, assuming that the propagation delay of every message sent from a correct process s_i to another correct process s_j is at most one time unit.

We sometimes refer to latency of k time units as k *message delays*.

We also speak about *common-case latency*; as detailed later, this is the worst case number of time units measured not over all possible executions, but rather over a subset of executions that satisfy certain constraints.

2.4 READ/WRITE STORAGE

Definition 2.10 Storage A distributed read/write storage (or, simply, storage, also called a *register* [Lamport, 1986]) is a shared object consisting of the following:

1. set of values D, and a special value $\perp \notin D$ (called the initial value);

2. two operations:

   (a) $write(v)$, with argument $v \in D$, and

   (b) $read()$;

3. set of responses $D \cup \{\perp, ack\}$;

4. sequential specification of storage is any sequence of read/write operations such that the responses of operations comply with the following:

   (a) $write(v) \triangleq x \leftarrow v$; return ack (where x is initialized to $\perp$)

   (b) $read() \triangleq$ return x.

Storage implementations. Storage object may be implemented either in the message-passing or in the shared memory model. In this monograph we focus solely on *wait-free* [Herlihy, 1991] storage algorithms.

Definition 2.11 Wait-Freedom A storage algorithm satisfies *wait-freedom* if and only if every read/write operation invoked by a correct process eventually completes.

In other words, wait-freedom is a *liveness* property [Alpern and Schneider, 1985] of storage emulations we are interested in.

A storage algorithm execution ex is said to be *well-formed* if: (a) no benign process c invokes a new operation in ex before all operations previously invoked by c have completed in ex, and (b) no operation completes at a benign process before it is invoked. In this monograph we consider only well-formed executions. An operation op is said to be *pending* in an execution ex, if ex contains the invocation step of op, but not its response step.

A *history* of a (partial) execution is a sequence of invocation and response steps of read or write operations in the same order as they appear in the (partial) execution. We say that a history $H1$ *completes* history $H2$ if $H1$ can be obtained through the following modification of $H2$: for each incomplete invocation step sp in $H2$, either sp is removed from $H2$, or any valid matching response for that invocation is appended to the end of $H2$.

Moreover, we say that a complete operation op *precedes* an operation op' (or, alternatively, that op' *follows* op) in execution ex (these definitions also extend to execution histories) if the response step for op precedes the invocation step of op' in ex; we denote this by $op \leadsto_{ex} op'$[1]. Let op and op' be two invoked operation in ex; if neither $op \leadsto_{ex} op'$), nor $op' \leadsto_{ex} op$), we say that op and op' are *concurrent* (in ex). In addition, we say that an operation op is *uncontended* if op is not concurrent with any write operation. We also say that op is *synchronous* if the system is synchronous during the interval between the invocation and completion of op.

We assume a special write operation called an *initial write*, denoted by wr_0, that writes the initial value $\perp$ to the register. By convention, the initial $write$ precedes all other operations in every execution.

Common-case latency. The common-case latency of $read$ and $write$ operations is defined as the worst case number of time units that an uncontended synchronous operation takes to complete.

Storage consistency semantics. In this monograph we consider the classical storage consistency semantics, namely *safe*, *regular* and *atomic* storage, that were introduced in [Lamport, 1986]. A storage algorithm A is safe (resp., regular, atomic), if every execution of A satisfies *safeness* (resp., *regularity*, *atomicity*). These consistency properties represent different *safety* properties [Alpern and Schneider, 1985] of storage emulations in which we are interested.

[1] Index ex is omitted when the execution is evident from the context.

We first define a useful notion of a last write preceding a read. Then, we give definitions of *safeness*, *regularity* and *atomicity*.

Definition 2.12 Last write preceding a read Given an execution ex and a read rd in ex, write wr is the *last write preceding* rd (in ex), if:

- $wr \leadsto rd$, and
- there is no $wr' \neq wr$ such that $wr \leadsto wr'$ and $wr' \leadsto rd$.

Assuming well-formed operations, it is not difficult to see that Definition 2.12 uniquely defines a last preceding write in the single-writer context, where only one process is allowed to invoke write operations. We use Definition 2.12 to define safeness and regularity which, in turn, apply only to the single writer setting.

Definition 2.13 Safeness A (partial) execution satisfies *safeness* if every uncontended read rd operation returns the value written by the last write that precedes rd.

Remark 2.14 Notice that safeness allows a read concurrent with a write to return any value.

Definition 2.15 Regularity A (partial) execution satisfying safeness satisfies *regularity* if, additionally, every contended read returns a value written by one of the concurrent writes or the value written by the last preceding write.

Finally, we define the *atomicity* property which applies to both single writer and multi-writer settings. Roughly speaking, an execution ex satisfies atomicity if ex satisfies regularity and *read inversion* does not occur in ex, i.e., if a read rd' follows some other read rd, then rd' does not return an older value than rd. More formally (see also Lemma 13.16 of [Lynch, 1996]):

Definition 2.16 Atomicity Denote by Π_H the set of all operations in a given history H. A (partial) execution satisfies *atomicity*, if for every history H' of any of its partial executions, there is a history H that completes H' and an irreflexive partial ordering $\prec$ on Π_H, such that:
(A1) if $op1$ precedes $op2$ in H then it is not the case that $op2 \prec op1$;
(A2) if $op1$ is a write operation in Π_H and $op2$ is any other operation in Π_H, then either $op1 \prec op2$ or $op2 \prec op1$; and
(A3) the value returned by each read operation is the value written by the last preceding write operation according to $\prec$.[2]

[2]Notice that the value returned by a read might be $\perp$ in case the initial write is the last preceding write according to $\prec$.

2.5 CONSENSUS

Our consensus framework applies to the message-passing model and divides the set of processes into three sets: *proposers*, *acceptors* and *learners* [Lamport, 1998]. These sets are not strictly disjoint: a single process can play more than one role. Most often, a replica in a practical system plays all three roles at the same time. Other popular deployments involve clients acting as proposers and servers as acceptors and learners. As we already mentioned, all processes are interconnected with point-to-point communication channels.

Roughly, proposers propose values that are to be agreed upon by learners, where the role of acceptors is to help learners agree. Consensus exports one operation: propose(v), that can be invoked only by proposers (we say that a proposer p *proposes* v), whereas it returns a value at every learner (we say that a learner l *learns* v). We assume that every proposer p is initialized with a single proposal value. Unlike in other consensus variants, we do not require every proposer to propose a value; however, a proposer can propose a value at most once.

Definition 2.17 Consensus An algorithm A solves consensus if every (partial) execution of A satisfies the following properties.

- *(Validity)* If a benign learner learns a value v and all proposers are benign, then some proposer proposed v;
- *(Agreement)* No two benign learners learn different values;
- *(Termination)* If a correct proposer proposes a value, then eventually, every correct learner learns a value.

In this monograph, we will largely focus on the *safety* properties of consensus, i.e., Validity and Agreement. Our focus on safety (consistency) properties of consensus is driven by the desire to emphasize roles of different quorum systems which are best observed on the consistency level.

In order to satisfy consensus *liveness*, i.e., the *Termination* property, timing relaxation is needed since the asynchronous consensus with faulty processes is impossible [Fischer et al., 1985]. For simplicity and clarity, we abstract out the reasoning about Termination by using certain classes of failure detectors [Chandra and Toueg, 1995] as abstractions.

In particular, we rely on the class of *eventual leader* failure detectors, denoted by Ω and implementable in eventually synchronous systems, defined earlier. Informally, Ω provides each process with an idea of a leader process, such that, eventually, all correct processes agree on the identity of the same correct process being the leader. Ω is more formally defined as follows [Raynal, 2010].

Definition 2.18 Eventual leader failure detector Given a set of processes S, Ω is a shared object exporting one operation $leader()$ which returns process ID $s_i \in S$. Denote the response to invocation of $leader()$ by process $s_i \in S$ at time τ by $leader_i^{\tau}$. Then, Ω is defined by the following properties:

- *(Leader validity)* $\forall s_i \in S, \forall \tau : leader_i^\tau \in S$;
- *(Eventual leadership)* $\exists s_j \in alive(S), \exists \tau : \forall \tau' \geq \tau : \forall s_i \in alive(S) : leader_i^{\tau'} = s_j$.

Notice that for an arbitrarily long and unknown (yet finite) period of time, Ω may output different leaders at different processes. These transient leaders might as well be faulty processes. However, Ω guarantees to eventually return a single correct process as the leader.

Although quorums often play an important role in failure detector implementations (including those of Ω as well), these implementations remain out of the scope of this monograph. Failure detectors and their implementations are described in detail in another lecture that appears in this series [Raynal, 2010].

2.6 PSEUDOCODE CONVENTIONS

Throughout this monograph we present several storage and consensus algorithm both in shared memory and message passing models. This monograph uses algorithm notation similar to standard textbooks (e.g., [Cachin et al., 2011]).

Notably, the pseudocode specifies actions, both internal and external output ones, that a (correct) process performs in response to: (a) an external input action; (b) a specific condition evaluated on the internal state; or (c) a combination of an input action and an internal state condition. This is captured by an **upon** statement and depicted in Algorithm 1.

Algorithm 1 upon statement

Local variables initialization: $localState \leftarrow initState$

upon external input event **or** $condition(localState)$ **do**
    perform a sequence internal and/or external output actions
end upon

We assume that every process executes the code inside **upon** statements in a mutually exclusive way. This implies that the same process does not handle two inputs or state transitions concurrently. Notice, however, that the execution of the code within the **upon** statement is not atomic since processes can fail during execution of a given statement, or in between two statements. Once the code within a specific **upon** statement is executed, the process keeps checking (implicitly) whether any other **upon** statement can be executed. We assume that this periodic checking is *fair*, i.e., that an enabled **upon** statement will eventually be executed by a correct process.

Finally, and for simpler algorithm notation, we introduce one exception to the concurrent execution of **upon** statements, using the **when** statement. Namely, **when** statement can be used to break the **upon** statement, while maintaining the better pseudocode structure. More concretely, in this monograph we assume that two pseudocode variants given in Algorithm 2 are equivalent.

Algorithm 2 when statement nested in **upon** and equivalent pseudocode

---

```
 1: upon A do
 2:     B
 3:     when C
 4:         D
 5:     end when
 6:     E
 7: end upon
```

```
 8: upon A do
 9:     B
10: end upon
11: upon C do
12:     D
13:     E
14: end upon
```

CHAPTER 3

Classical Quorum Systems

In this chapter, we first give basic definitions of the notions that evolve around quorum systems. This is followed by exemplifying some of the classical quorum systems used in distributed computing. Finally, we introduce some important quorum system measures.

3.1 BASICS

Definition 3.1 Set System Given a set S, a set system (or a hypergraph) $\boldsymbol{H}$ is a non-empty subset of the powerset of S, i.e., $\boldsymbol{H} \subseteq 2^S$.

In other words, a set system is a set of subsets of S.

Notation 3.2 We denote by $m(\boldsymbol{H})$ the minimal cardinality of some element in $\boldsymbol{H}$, i.e.,

$$m(\boldsymbol{H}) = \min_{Q \in \boldsymbol{H}} |Q|.$$

Definition 3.3 Strategy Strategy σ is a probabilistic function that takes a (non-empty) set system $\boldsymbol{H}$ as input, and outputs some $Q \in \boldsymbol{H}$ with probability $\sigma_{\boldsymbol{H}}(Q)$, such that:

$$\sum_{Q \in \boldsymbol{H}} \sigma_{\boldsymbol{H}}(Q) = 1 .$$

The basic definition we use in this monograph is that of a quorum system.

Definition 3.4 Quorum System Given a set $S = \{s_1, s_2 \ldots s_n\}$ $(n \geq 1)$, a set system $\mathbf{QS}$ is a quorum system over S, if and only if

(Intersection) $\forall Q_1, Q_2 \in \mathbf{QS} : Q_1 \cap Q_2 \neq \emptyset$.

Elements of a quorum system are simply called *quorums*. When S is understood, we omit it for simplicity.

A related notion to quorum systems is a the notion of a *coterie* ('exclusive groups') [Garcia-Molina and Barbara, 1985]. Coteries are quorum systems with the minimality property stating that there are no two quorums such that one is the strict subset of the other.

Definition 3.5 Coterie A quorum system (over set S) QS is a coterie, if and only if

(Minimality) $\forall Q_1, Q_2 \in \boldsymbol{QS} : Q_1 \not\subset Q_2$.

Definition 3.6 Let $\boldsymbol{C}$ and $\boldsymbol{C'}$ be coteries over the same set S. Then, $\boldsymbol{C}$ dominates $\boldsymbol{C'}$ if:

$$\boldsymbol{C} \neq \boldsymbol{C'} \text{ and } C' \in \boldsymbol{C'}, \exists C \in \boldsymbol{C} : C \subseteq C' .$$

Notation 3.7 If a coterie C dominates coterie C', we write $C \prec C'$.

Given the relation *dominates*, we define dominated and non-dominated coteries.

Definition 3.8 A coterie C' is *dominated* if there exists a coterie C such that $C \prec C'$. Otherwise, C' is called *non-dominated.*

Notation 3.9 We denote the class of all non dominated coteries by NDC.

A fundamental refinement of quorum systems is the one which distinguishes between read and write quorums [Gifford, 1979]. We refer to such quorum system variation as *asymmetric read/write (R/W) quorum systems.*

Definition 3.10 Asymmetric R/W Quorum System Given a set $S = \{s_1, s_2 \ldots s_n\}$ $(n \geq 1)$, and two set systems **RQ** and **WQ** over S, the union **AQS** = **RQ** ∪ **WQ** is an asymmetric read/write (R/W) quorum system, if and only if

(Asymmetric Intersection) $\forall Q_1 \in \mathbf{RQ}, \forall Q_2 \in \mathbf{WQ} : Q_1 \cap Q_2 \neq \emptyset$.

In the following, we briefly instantiate classical quorum systems through few examples.

3.2 EXAMPLES

Singleton. The simplest quorum system is the one containing a singleton: $\boldsymbol{Singl} = \{\{s_i\}\}$, for some $s_i \in S$. Notice that $\boldsymbol{QS} = \{\emptyset\}$ is not a quorum system since it fails to satisfy the Intersection property.

Majorities. Arguably the most frequently used quorum system is a Majority coterie.

$$\boldsymbol{Maj} = \{Q \subseteq S : |Q| = \lceil \tfrac{n+1}{2} \rceil\}.$$

Finite projective planes (FPP). If set S contains $n = k^2 + k + 1$ nodes, where k is a prime power, then a finite projective plane of order k is a quorum system, in which every quorum has exactly $k + 1 = O(\sqrt{n})$ nodes, every node is contained in exactly $k + 1$ quorums and every two quorums intersect in exactly one node. The simplest example of an FPP quorum system is given by Fano plane, an order 2 FPP over a set of $n = 7$ nodes (see Fig. 3.1).

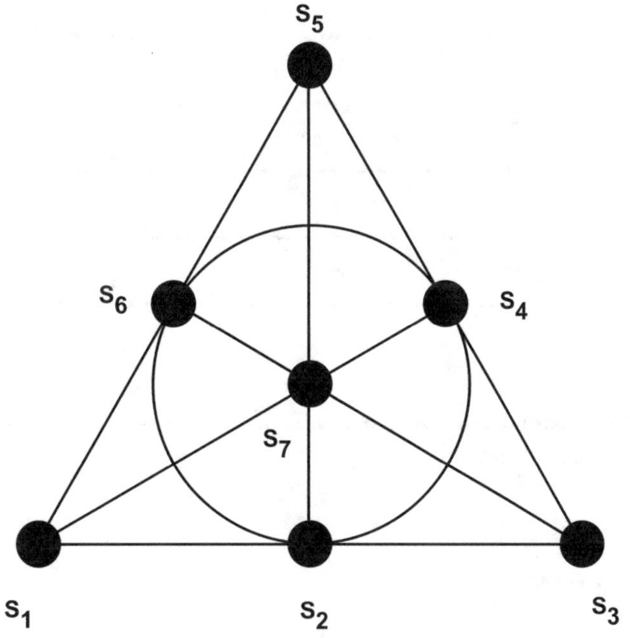

Figure 3.1: Fano plane (an order 2 FPP).

Grid. Assume $|S| = k^2$, for some integer k and nodes arranged in a square matrix (i.e., a grid). Then, a set of subsets of S of the form $Q_{i,j}$, such that each $Q_{i,j}$ contains all elements in row i and column j $(1 \leq i, j \leq k)$ forms the quorum system over S. Such a quorum system has $k^2 = n$ quorums, each of size $2k - 1 = O(\sqrt{n})$ and every quorum intersects with every other quorum in at least 2 nodes.

To minimize the size of quorum intersection we can construct a slightly different quorum system containing $k = \sqrt{n}$ quorums Q_i $(1 \leq i \leq k)$ such that Q_i contains all nodes from row i and exactly one node from each row $j > i$ [Malkhi]. It is not difficult to see that the quorum size in this quorum system (we refer to as the Grid) remains $O(\sqrt{n})$, whereas the size of pair-wise intersections among quorums is 1.

B-Grid. A generalized grid-like quorum system, called B-Grid assumes a rectangular grid of R rows and c columns, such that rows are grouped into b bands of r rows ($R = br$), where band j ($1 \le j \le b$) contains rows $(j-1)r + 1 \dots jr$. Moreover, denote the intersection of column c and band j as *mini-column* (c, j). Then, the B-grid quorum system consists of b quorums Q_j ($1 \le j \le b$), each containing one mini-column from each band (i.e., b mini-columns (c_i, i), where $1 \le i \le b$ and $1 \le c_i \le c$) and one node from each column in band j (see also Fig. 3.2). It is not difficult to see that B-Grid is a quorum system in which every quorum contains exactly $br + c - 1$ nodes.

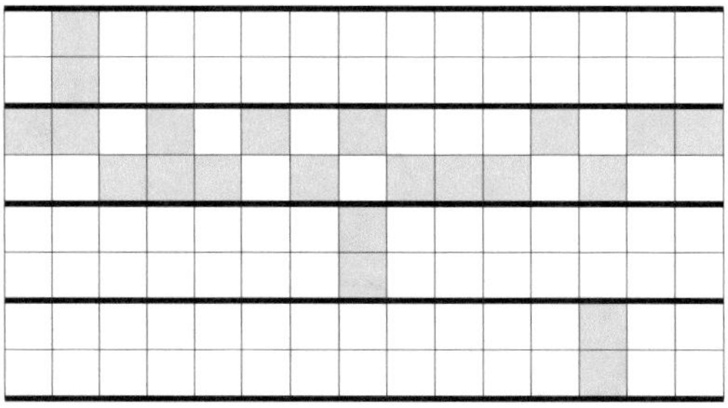

Figure 3.2: The B-Grid quorum system over a set of $n = brc = 120$ nodes, with $c = 15$ columns, $b = 4$ bands and $r = 2$ rows per band.

3.3 MEASURES

Two fundamental quorum system measures are *load* and *availability*.

3.3.1 LOAD

3.3.1.1 Definition

In principle, a protocol using a quorum system will need to access at least one quorum. In the best case, a process accessing a quorum will be able to select a given quorum Q and access all nodes that belong to Q. Such usage of a quorum system will induce *load*, which, in short, measures the minimal access probability of the busiest node in the system. The load measures the quality of a quorum system: low load translates to the busiest node being accessed rarely, which allows it to perform other, unrelated tasks. Intuitively, the lower the load of a quorum system, the better.

With each strategy, there is an associated load induced on each node as well as the load on the entire quorum system. Given strategy σ, the load on a given node s_i is the probability that s_i will belong to a quorum selected according to strategy σ. The load of σ on a quorum system is defined as the *maximum* load of each individual node. Finally, the *(system) load of a quorum system* is the *minimum* load across all possible strategies [Naor and Wool, 1998].

Definition 3.11 Load Let $\boldsymbol{QS}$ be the quorum system over S. Then, we define the following.

1. Load induced by strategy σ on node $s_i \in S$: $l_\sigma(s_i, \boldsymbol{QS}) = \sum_{Q \ni s_i} \sigma_{\boldsymbol{QS}}(Q)$.
2. Load induced by strategy σ on $\boldsymbol{QS}$: $\mathcal{L}_\sigma(\boldsymbol{QS}) = \max_{s_i \in S} l_\sigma(s_i, \boldsymbol{QS})$.
3. Load of $\boldsymbol{QS}$: $\mathcal{L}(\boldsymbol{QS}) = \min_\sigma \mathcal{L}_\sigma(\boldsymbol{QS})$ (minimum over all strategies σ).

Remark 3.12 It is very important to highlight that a load of a given quorum system is *independent* of any given protocol that might use this quorum system. On the other hand, a given protocol might come with a given strategy σ and the associated load induced by this strategy.

In a sense, the above definition of load is a best-case one because the connection between strategies and load assumes that a quorum selected by a strategy will always be accessed. The load definition does not account for possible failures and/or asynchrony, which may prevent a selected quorum from being accessed.

Clearly, calculating system load is a minimization problem subject to certain constraints related to our definition of strategies. Therefore, Definition 3.11 can be redefined as a linear program.

Definition 3.13 Let $\boldsymbol{QS} = \{Q_1 \dots Q_m\}$ be the quorum system over S. Define a variable σ_i for each quorum $Q \in \boldsymbol{QS}$ and an additional variable L. Then the system load is defined with the following linear program:

$$LOAD : \mathcal{L}(\boldsymbol{QS}) = \min L, \text{ s.t.} \begin{cases} \sum_{i=1}^{m} \sigma_i = 1 \\ \sum_{Q_i \ni s_j} \sigma_i \leq L, \forall s_j \in S \\ \sigma_i \geq 0, L \geq 0 \end{cases} .$$

It is also useful to state the dual linear program of $LOAD$. This will help us derive an important lower bound on system load.

Definition 3.14 Let $\boldsymbol{QS} = \{Q_1 \dots Q_m\}$ be the quorum system over S. Define a variable y_j for each element s_j of S and an additional variable T. The dual linear program of $LOAD$ is:

$$DLOAD : d(\boldsymbol{QS}) = \max D, \text{ s.t. } \begin{cases} \sum_{j=1}^{n} y_j \leq 1 \\ \sum_{s_j \in Q_i} y_j \geq D, \forall Q_i \in \boldsymbol{QS} \\ y_j \geq 0, D \neq 0 \end{cases} .$$

3.3.1.2 Lower Bound on System Load

We now prove an important lower bound on the load of *any* quorum system [Naor and Wool, 1998]. Namely, we show that $\mathcal{L}(\boldsymbol{QS}) \geq \max\left\{\frac{1}{m(\boldsymbol{QS})}, \frac{m(\boldsymbol{QS})}{n}\right\}$, which implies $\mathcal{L}(\mathbf{QS}) \geq 1/\sqrt{n}$.

Lemma 3.15 *Let $\boldsymbol{QS}$ be the quorum system over S. Let $0 \leq y_j \leq 1$ for all j, such that $s_j \in S$ and let $0 < d \leq 1$. If $\sum_{j=1}^{n} y_j = 1$ and $\sum_{s_j \in Q_i} y_j \geq d$ for all $Q_i \in \boldsymbol{QS}$, then $\mathcal{L}(\boldsymbol{QS}) \geq d$.*

Proof. It is straightforward to see that the vector $[y_1, \ldots, y_n, d]$ is a feasible point of $DLOAD$. The lemma follows by the weak duality theorem of linear programming (see, e.g., [Papadimitriou and Steiglitz, 1982]). □

Lemma 3.16 $\mathcal{L}(\boldsymbol{QS}) \geq \frac{m(\boldsymbol{QS})}{n}$ *for any quorum system $\boldsymbol{QS}$.*

Proof. Fix vector $[y_1 \ldots, y_n] = [1/n, \ldots, 1/n]$. By definition of $m(\boldsymbol{QS})$, for any $Q_i \in \boldsymbol{QS}$ we have $\sum_{s_j \in Q_i} y_j \geq \frac{m(\boldsymbol{QS})}{n}$. By Lemma 3.15, $\mathcal{L}(\boldsymbol{QS}) \geq \frac{m(\boldsymbol{QS})}{n}$. □

Lemma 3.17 $\mathcal{L}(\boldsymbol{QS}) \geq \frac{1}{m(\boldsymbol{QS})}$ *for any quorum system $\boldsymbol{QS}$.*

Proof. Fix $Q \in \boldsymbol{QS}$ such that $|Q| = m(\boldsymbol{QS})$. Fix vector $[y_1 \ldots, y_n]$ such that $y_j = \frac{1}{m(\boldsymbol{QS})}$, if $s_j \in Q$ and $y_j = 0$, otherwise. Clearly, for any $Q_i \in \boldsymbol{QS}$ we have $\sum_{s_j \in Q_i} y_j \geq \frac{1}{m(\boldsymbol{QS})}$. By Lemma 3.15, $\mathcal{L}(\boldsymbol{QS}) \geq \frac{1}{m(\boldsymbol{QS})}$. □

Theorem 3.18 $\mathcal{L}(\boldsymbol{QS}) \geq \frac{1}{\sqrt{n}}$ for any quorum system $\boldsymbol{QS}$.

Proof. If $m(\boldsymbol{QS}) \geq \frac{1}{\sqrt{n}}$, the Theorem follows from Lemma 3.16. On the other hand, if $m(\boldsymbol{QS}) \leq \frac{1}{\sqrt{n}}$, the theorem follows from Lemma 3.17. □

3.3.1.3 Capacity

Capacity is another measure of a quorum system, tightly related to the load. Intuitively, when a quorum is accessed each of the elements of that quorum become busy and cannot handle other concurrent accesses. Capacity is defined as the maximal rate at which the system can handle quorum accesses. Assuming a synchronous system in which every quorum access takes one time unit, a quorum system $\boldsymbol{QS}$ over S can handle a quorum accesses over a period of time t, if each element of S is accessed at most t times.

More formally, the number of quorum accesses can be defined as the following linear program.

Definition 3.19 A quorum system $\boldsymbol{QS}$ can handle $a(\boldsymbol{QS}, t)$ quorum accesses in time t, if there exist integers $accessCnt_Q$ for each $Q \in \boldsymbol{QS}$ such that:

$$QA : a(\boldsymbol{QS}, t) = \max \sum_{Q \in \boldsymbol{QS}} accessCnt_Q, \text{ s.t. } \begin{cases} \sum_{Q \ni s_i} accessCnt_Q \leq t, \forall s_i \in S \\ accessCnt_Q \geq 0, accessCnt_Q \in \mathbb{N} \end{cases} .$$

Then, the capacity is defined as the limit of the normalized number of accesses over long period of time.

Definition 3.20 $Cap(\boldsymbol{QS}) = \lim_{t \to \infty} \frac{a(\boldsymbol{QS},t)}{t}$.

However, if we have the information about the load of the quorum system, this already captures the information about capacity, as stipulated by the following theorem.

Theorem 3.21 $Cap(\mathbf{QS}) = 1/\mathcal{L}(\mathbf{QS})$.

We refer the reader interested in the proof of Theorem 3.21 to [Naor and Wool, 1998].

3.3.2 AVAILABILITY

Besides achieving consistency and lowering the cost of accessing replicated services, the goal of using quorum systems is also to increase the availability of replicated services. There are two basic availability measures: *resilience* and *failure probability*.

3.3.2.1 Resilience

A fundamental availability measure of quorum systems availability is the *resilience*, which is also sometimes referred to as *node vulnerability* [Barbara and Garcia-Molina, 1986] or *fault-tolerance*. The resilience is defined as follows:

Definition 3.22 The resilience $\mathcal{R}(\boldsymbol{QS})$ of a quorum system $\boldsymbol{QS}$ is the maximal integer t such that, despite a failure of any t processes in the system, there is a quorum $Q \in \mathbf{QS}$ such that no process belonging to Q fails.

Notice that the Intersection property implies $\mathcal{R}(\boldsymbol{QS}) < m(\boldsymbol{QS})$. Clearly, the failure of all nodes in any single quorum implies at least one node failure in every quorum. Therefore, the resilience is bounded by the minimal quorum cardinality — $m(\boldsymbol{QS})$.

Of particular importance are *optimally resilient* quorum systems. It is straightforward to show, starting from the Intersection property, that no quorum system can have a resilience greater than $\left\lfloor \frac{n-1}{2} \right\rfloor$. This is exactly the resilience of a majority coterie.

We also introduce the notion of t-resilience, very often used to characterize quorum systems and algorithms that rely upon them.

Definition 3.23 Quorum system $\boldsymbol{QS}$ is t-resilient if and only if $\mathcal{R}(\boldsymbol{QS}) \geq t$.

Finally, the definition of resilience can be extended beyond threshold failures to set system resilience [Bazzi, 2001].

Definition 3.24 Quorum system $\mathbf{QS}$ is *resilient to set system* $\boldsymbol{F}$, if and only if $\forall F \in \mathbf{F}, \exists Q \in \mathbf{QS}$: $Q \cap F = \emptyset$.

3.3.3 FAILURE PROBABILITY

Global failure probability, or simply *failure probability* [Peleg and Wool, 1995] is defined assuming independent process failures in the uniform probabilistic fault model. In short, failure probability $F_p(\mathbf{QS})$ is the probability that no quorum in $\mathbf{QS}$ will have a non-faulty node, where p is the probability of failure of each of the nodes in S. In a sense, since the failure probability is not expressing availability, but rather its dual, it is also known as *non-availability*. More formally:

Definition 3.25 Given the probability p uniformly distributed over the set of processes S and a quorum system $\boldsymbol{QS}$ over S, denote by $F_p(Q)$ the probability that some node in $Q \in \boldsymbol{QS}$ fails. Then, failure probability is defined as:

$$F_p(\mathbf{QS}) = \prod_{Q \in \mathbf{QS}} F_p(Q).$$

In general, quorum system $\mathbf{QS}$ is considered to have good failure probability if $F_p(\mathbf{QS})$ tends to 0 for large values of n assuming $p < 1/2$.

The two availability measures, resilience and failure probability , are related. Namely, it can be shown that $F_p(\mathbf{QS})$ is at least $e^{-\Omega(\mathcal{R}(\mathbf{QS}))}$ [Peleg and Wool, 1995]. Moreover, since $\mathcal{R}(\mathbf{QS}) < m(\mathbf{QS})$ and $m(\mathbf{QS}) \leq n\mathcal{L}(\mathbf{QS})$, the tradeoff between resilience and load is expressed as $\mathcal{R}(\mathbf{QS}) < n\mathcal{L}(\mathbf{QS})$. Finally, we can express the tradeoff between the failure probability and the load [Naor and Wool, 1998]. Clearly, the failure probability is at least the probability that all the nodes from the quorum containing the smallest number of nodes fail, i.e., $F_p(\mathbf{QS}) \geq p^{m(\mathbf{QS})} \geq p^{n\mathcal{L}(\mathbf{QS})}$.

3.3.4 COMPARISON

In Table 3.1 we overview the quality measures of the quorum systems presented in Sec. 3.2 [Malkhi, Naor and Wool, 1998].

QS	$\mathcal{L}(\mathbf{QS})$	$\mathcal{R}(\mathbf{QS})$	$F_p(\mathbf{QS})$
Singleton	1	0	p
Majorities	$\lceil \frac{n+1}{2} \rceil$	$\lfloor \frac{n-1}{2} \rfloor$	$e^{-\Omega(n)}$
FPP	$O(\frac{1}{\sqrt{n}})$	$O(\sqrt{n})$	1*
Grid	$O(\frac{1}{\sqrt{n}})$	$O(\sqrt{n})$	1*
B-Grid	$O(\frac{1}{\sqrt{n}})$	$O(\sqrt{n})$	$O(e^{-\frac{n^{1/4}}{2}})$

* For large values of n.

Singleton is interesting when the individual node probability failure is high ($p > 1/2$), when this simple quorum system offers the best failure probability. Otherwise, (assuming $p < 1/2$), Majorities has the best availability but poor load. On the other hand, FPP and Grid have optimal load, yet their failure probability is poor for large value of n. This is corrected by B-Grid, which has asymptotically optimal failure probability. The data in Table 3.1 for B-Grid are given assuming $c = \sqrt{n}, r = ln(c)$ and $p \leq \frac{1}{3}$.

Other quorum systems that combine optimal load with optimal failure probability include CWalls [Peleg and Wool, 1997], Paths [Naor and Wool, 1998], and Triangle Lattice [Bazzi, 2000a].

3.4 BIBLIOGRAPHIC NOTES

- For a comprehensive survey of early approaches to consistency using quorum systems, the reader is referred to [Davidson et al., 1985].

- The finite projective planes quorum system was first used in [Maekawa, 1985] in a mutual exclusion algorithm.

- The first grid-like quorum system was used in the replication protocol of [Cheung et al., 1992]. The B-Grid quorum system was proposed in [Naor and Wool, 1998].
- Load and availability were first studied in [Naor and Wool, 1998] and [Peleg and Wool, 1995], respectively.

CHAPTER 4

Classical Quorum-Based Emulations

Throughout this monograph we present several storage and consensus emulations that are based on specific quorum systems satisfying particular properties. This notion of an implementation based on a given quorum system is captured as follows.

Definition 4.1 A storage (resp., consensus) emulation is *based* on a quorum system $\mathcal{QS}$ if it the emulation satisfies:

- safety properties in all executions, and
- liveness properties in all executions in which at least one quorum $Q \in \mathcal{QS}$ is available.

In this chapter, we give examples of classical storage and consensus emulations based on classical quorum systems defined in Chapter 3.

First, we focus on the static quorum membership, where the underlying quorum system does not change during the execution of the storage/consensus protocol. The emulations we show in this monograph are based on the celebrated ABD storage emulation [Attiya et al., 1995] (Sec. 4.1) and the Synod consensus algorithm of the Paxos state-machine replication protocol [Lamport, 1998] (Sec. 4.2). Throughout this monograph, we will be often coming back to these fundamental emulations, showing how they can be adapted to various refinements of the classical quorum system notion.

Later in this chapter, in Sec. 4.3 we turn to dynamic network membership where the changes in the underlying set of participating processes and quorums themselves are allowed. In this context, we present the basic principles of the RAMBO dynamic storage protocol [Gilbert et al., 2010], which relies on the ABD and Paxos/Synod protocols developed beforehand.

Emulations we present in this chapter assume the asynchronous message-passing communication model. Moreover, emulations in Secs. 4.2 and 4.3 assume the eventual leader failure detector Ω. Finally, in this chapter, we assume that processes mail fail only by crashing.

4.1 STORAGE EMULATION

Classical quorum systems have been extensively used in the context of storage simulations in message-passing systems. The seminal example is the ABD asynchronous atomic storage emulation [Attiya et al., 1995].

4.1.1 THE SETUP

Here, we consider a generalized multi-writer multi-reader quorum-based variant of the ABD distributed storage algorithm — the shared object implemented by the algorithm is referred to as ABD. We assume two possibly distinct, finite sets of processes: the set of *clients*, denoted by C and the set of *servers*, denoted by S. Furthermore, we assume that each client has unique ID c, taken from the set of natural numbers (i.e., $c \in \mathbb{N}$), whereas servers are denoted by $s_1, s_2, \ldots, s_n$. Any client or server may fail by crashing.

We further assume an asymmetric read/write quorum system $\boldsymbol{AQS}$ over S such that $\boldsymbol{AQS}$ is known to clients, along with the corresponding sets of read and write quorums, $\boldsymbol{RQ} \subseteq \boldsymbol{AQS}$ and $\boldsymbol{WQ} \subseteq \boldsymbol{AQS}$ (see Definition 3.10). ABD is based on $\boldsymbol{AQS}$, i.e., it is required to satisfy atomicity in all executions (i.e., despite the failure of any number of clients/servers), as well as wait-freedom as long as there are at least one read quorum and one write quorum that contain correct servers. In other words, ABD is wait-free as long as there are quorums $Q_R \in \boldsymbol{RQ}$ and $Q_W \in \boldsymbol{WQ}$ such that in every point in every execution $Q_R \subseteq alive(S)$ and $Q_W \subseteq alive(S)$.

4.1.2 THE ALGORITHM

The full generalized ABD algorithm, briefly described below, is given as Algorithm 3 (client pseudocode) and Algorithm 4 (server pseudocode).

Both reads and writes proceed in two phases, each ending with a confirmation that at least one quorum was accessed. In the first phase of a write (the Timestamp synchronization phase), a client (a writer) first contacts a read quorum in order to determine the highest timestamp $maxts$ used prior to the current write (lines 3-7, Algorithm 3). Then, in the second phase (the Write phase), after incrementing timestamp $maxts$ locally, the writer propagates the written value, along with the timestamp and its own ID c within a $write$ message to a write quorum (line 9, Algorithm 3).

Similarly, in the first phase of a read operation (the Read phase), a client (a reader) retrieves the value associated with the highest timestamp reported by a read quorum (lines 16-22, Algorithm 3). In determining the highest timestamp, writers' IDs serve as tiebreakers (line 20, Algorithm 3). Then, in the second phase, the reader propagates the read value along with its timestamp to a write quorum (this phase is called the Writeback phase, lines 23-27, Algorithm 3).

The server code is straightforward (Algorithm 4). Server s_i maintains two variables: (1) val_i, the local storage value at s_i, and (2) tag_i, which is a pair holding the timestamp $tag_i.ts$ and the client ID $tag_i.cid$ associated with val_i. More specifically (assuming written values do not repeat, for simplicity), $tag_i.ts$ is the timestamp used by writer c in the $write$ message of the $write$ operation that initially wrote val_i, whereas $tag_i.cid$ is precisely the ID of this writer, c.

Servers update locally stored variables when they receive a $write$ message with a value associated with a higher timestamp then they locally store, where client IDs used as tiebreakers. Notice that this $write$ message might be received from a writer, but also from a reader executing the Writeback phase.

Algorithm 3 Generalized ABD algorithm (client c pseudocode)

Local variables initialization: $opCnt \leftarrow 0; maxts \leftarrow 0; maxcid \leftarrow 0; maxval \leftarrow \perp$

1: **upon** $inv_c(ABD, write(v))$ **do**
2:     $opCnt \leftarrow opCnt + 1$
3:     **Phase 1:**   *{Timestamp synchronization}*
4:         $send\ (read, opCnt)$ to all servers
5:         **when** $receive\ (readack, val_i, \langle ts_i, cid_i \rangle, opCnt)$ from all s_i from some $Q \in \boldsymbol{RQ}$
6:             $maxts \leftarrow$ maximum ts_i in received $readack$ messages
7:         **end when**
8:     **Phase 2:**   *{Write}*
9:         $send\ (write, v, \langle maxts + 1, c \rangle, opCnt)$ to all servers
10:         **when** $receive\ (writeack, opCnt)$ from all s_i from some $Q \in \boldsymbol{WQ}$
11:             **return** $resp_c(ABD, ack)$
12:         **end when**
13: **end upon**

14: **upon** $inv_c(ABD, read())$ **do**
15:     $opCnt \leftarrow opCnt + 1$
16:     **Phase 1:**   *{Read}*
17:         $send\ (read, opCnt)$ to all servers
18:         **when** $receive\ (readack, val_i, \langle ts_i, cid_i \rangle, opCnt)$ from all s_i from some $Q \in \boldsymbol{RQ}$
19:             $maxts \leftarrow$ maximum ts_i in received $readack$ messages
20:             $maxcid \leftarrow$ maximum cid_i in received $readack$ messages with $maxts$
21:             $maxval \leftarrow val_i$ in received $readack$ message with $\langle maxts, maxcid \rangle$
22:         **end when**
23:     **Phase 2:**   *{Writeback}*
24:         $send\ (write, maxval, \langle maxts, maxcid \rangle, opCnt)$ to all servers
25:         **when** $receive\ (writeack, opCnt)$ from all s_i from some $Q \in \boldsymbol{WQ}$
26:             **return** $resp_c(ABD, maxval)$
27:         **end when**
28: **end upon**

Algorithm 4 Generalized ABD algorithm (server s_i pseudocode)

Local variables initialization: $tag_i[ts, cid] = \langle 0, 0\rangle$; $val_i \leftarrow \perp$

---

upon *receive* $(read, cnt)$ from client c **do**
  $send(readack, val_i, tag_i, cnt)$ to c
end upon

upon *receive* $(write, val', \langle ts', cid'\rangle, cnt)$ from client c **do**
  if $ts' > tag_i.ts$ **or** $(ts' = tag_i.ts$ **and** $cid' > tag_i.cid)$ **then**
    $tag_i \leftarrow \langle ts', cid'\rangle$; $val_i \leftarrow val'$
  end if
  $send(writeack, cnt)$ to c
end upon

4.1.3 CORRECTNESS ARGUMENTS

It is straightforward to see that the ABD emulation satisfies wait-freedom as long as there are at least one read quorum and one write quorum that contain correct processes.

On the other hand, showing that ABD ensures consistency is more involved and this, not surprisingly, involves reasoning about quorum intersections. ABD consistency semantics is the strongest one — atomicity.

To sketch the proof of atomicity, notice again that the main feature of ABD, is that both *read* and *write* require two phases, with (at least) one quorum access in each phase. The intuition behind this is not entirely obvious. It is rather intuitive that the writers should write to a write quorum (Phase 2 of *write*) and that the readers should read from a read quorum (Phase 1 of *read*) — the non empty intersection between any read and write quorum (Def. 3.10) guarantees that the *read* will not miss a value written by a complete *write*. However, the answers to two questions are less obvious: (1) Why do writers read (Phase 1 of *write* — the Timestamp synchronization phase); and (2) why do readers write (Phase 2 of *read* - the Writeback phase)?

The Timestamp synchronization phase is there to facilitate ABD to a multi-writer setting, i.e., when there is more than one client invoking *write*. Namely, in a multi-writer setting, writers need to synchronize the timestamps, i.e., the timestamps should reflect the real-time order of non-concurrent *write* operations. To this end, in the Timestamp synchronization phase, a writer reads the highest timestamp used in *write* operations that precede the current *write*. In order to achieve this, writers make use of quorums. Namely, in the Timestamp synchronization phase a writer reads from a read quorum — a non-empty intersection between a read and a write quorum guarantees that the writer will be informed about all the timestamps propagated by preceding *write* operations within the corresponding Write phase. Notice that in a special case of a single-writer, the Timestamp synchronization phase in generalized ABD can be safely omitted[1]; in this case, the single writer can simply use its operation identifier $opCnt$ in place of $maxts + 1$ when sending the $write$.

Much as the Timestamp synchronization phase ensures consistent ordering of $write$ operations issued by different writers, the Writeback phase ensures consistency, or, more precisely, atomicity, among pairs of readers. To see this, observe that a reader could select the latest value in the Phase 1 of $read$ by solely relying on the information received from a single server. Due to the crashes of the writer, or servers, this information about the latest value might not have been propagated to a write quorum by the end of the Phase 1 of a given $read$. Hence, in order to inform the readers that invoke the following $read$ operations, a reader executes the Writeback phase, by propagating the read information to a write quorum. The writeback phase is critical in ensuring atomicity; however, it is not necessary to achieve weaker storage consistency semantics — regularity. Namely, in case of a regular variant of ABD, the readers can safely skip the Writeback phase and return $maxval$ right after the completion of Phase 1.

As we can see on the example of the ABD Writeback phase, consistency impacts latency. In a sense, in order to have atomic semantics instead of weaker regular one, ABD pays the price of additional round-trip between a reader and the servers. This observation was an important driver to the invention of latency-efficient quorum systems that we will discuss in more details in Chapter 6.

The following lemma proves that ABD is atomic.

Lemma 4.2 ABD Atomicity *The ABD algorithm given in Algorithms 3 and 4 satisfies atomicity in every execution.*

Proof. *Sketch.* Given history H'_{ex} of execution ex we define history H_{ex} that completes H'_{ex} as follows: (a) for any incomplete $write$ wr in H'_{ex} in which the writer completes the Timestamp synchronization phase, we append the response step for wr to the end of H'_{ex}; and (b) for any other incomplete operation op (including all incomplete $read$ operations) in H'_{ex}, we remove the invocation step of op from H'_{ex}.

We prove atomicity by establishing the partial order relation $\prec$ among all (complete) operations in H_{ex}, that satisfies the properties required by Definition 2.16.

In the case of ABD, defining $\prec$ is rather simple. Given any execution, we assign to each operation op a tag which consists of a pair $tag_{op} = \langle ts_{op}, cid_{op} \rangle$. We distinguish two cases.

- If op is a $write$, then ts_{op} equals the timestamp $maxts + 1$, where $maxts$ is computed by the writer in the Timestamp synchronization phase, i.e., $ts_{op} = maxts + 1$. Moreover, cid_{op} is the ID of the writer that executes the $write$ op.
- If op is a $read$ then ts_{op} (resp., cid_{op}) equals $maxts$ (resp., $maxcid$) computed by the reader in line 19 (resp., line 20) in Algorithm 3. Notice that, in this case, cid_{op} is the ID of the writer that wrote the value the reader is about to writeback and return.

[1]This is precisely the case in the original ABD algorithm [Attiya et al., 1995].

Moreover, by convention, the tag of the initial $write$ wr_0 is $tag_{wr_0} = \langle 0, 0 \rangle$.

We establish lexicographical ordering of tags, i.e., we write $tag_{op1} < tag_{op2}$, if and only if $ts_{op1} < ts_{op2}$ or $ts_{op1} = ts_{op2} \wedge cid_{op1} < cid_{op2}$.

Then we define $\prec$ based on tag ordering. More specifically, $op1 \prec op2$ if and only if:

- $op1$ is a $write$ and $op2$ is a $read$ and $tag_{op1} \leq tag_{op2}$; or
- $op1$ and $op2$ are the operations of the same type (i.e., both are $write$, or both are $read$ operations) or $op1$ is a $read$ and $op2$ is a $write$, and $tag_{op1} < tag_{op2}$.

We now prove that $\prec$ satisfies properties (A1)-(A3) of Definition 2.16. Since (A3) follows directly from our definition of $\prec$, we focus on proving properties (A1) and (A2).

(A1). To prove (A1) we show that if $op1$ precedes $op2$ in H_{ex}, then it is not the case that $op2 \prec op1$. First, we observe that, by construction of H_{ex}, if $op1$ precedes any operation in H_{ex} than $op1$ is complete in execution ex.

Since $op1$ completes before $op2$ is invoked, $op1$ completes the Write (resp., Writeback) phase in case $op1$ is a $write$ (resp., $read$) propagating its tag to a write quorum Q_w of servers before $op2$ is invoked. Hence, by the time $op2$ is invoked every server $s_i \in Q_w$ has locally the tag $\langle ts_i, cid_i \rangle \geq tag_{op1} = \langle ts_{op1}, cid_{op1} \rangle$. We distinguish two cases.

1. Operation $op2$ is a $write$ operation. Then, since $op1$ precedes $op2$ in H_{ex}, we argue that $tag_{op1} < tag_{op2}$.

   Since $op_2 \in H_{ex}$, op_2 completes the Timestamp synchronization phase, and obtains the tags from all servers from a read quorum Q_r of servers and selects the highest timestamp $maxts$. Then, since $Q_r \cap Q_w \neq \emptyset$ (Def. 3.10), we have $maxts \geq ts_{op1}$. Finally, since $ts_{op2} = maxts + 1$, we have $ts_{op2} > ts_{op1}$, which implies $tag_{op1} < tag_{op2}$. Hence, $op2 \prec op1$ does not hold.

2. Operation $op2$ is a $read$ operation. Then, since $op1$ precedes $op2$ in H_{ex}, we argue that $tag_{op1} \geq tag_{op2}$.

   Since $op_2 \in H_{ex}$, $op2$ completes the Read phase, and obtains the tags from all servers from a read quorum Q_r of servers and selects the highest timestamp $maxts$ and the highest client ID $maxcid$ associated with $maxts$. Then, since $Q_r \cap Q_w \neq \emptyset$ (Def. 3.10), we have $maxts \geq ts_{op1}$, as well as $maxcid \geq cid_{op1}$ in case $maxts = ts_{op1}$. Hence, $tag_{op1} \leq tag_{op2}$. Moreover, since $op2$ is a $read$, $op2 \prec op1$ does not hold.

(A2). To show property (A2) we show that if $op1$ is a $write$ operation in H_{ex} and $op2$ is any other operation in H_{ex}, then either $op1 \prec op2$ or $op2 \prec op1$. To show this, it is sufficient to show that the property holds if $op2$ is a $write$. The case where $op2$ is a $read$ follows directly from the definition of $\prec$.

By definition of $\prec$, in case $op2$ is a $write$, it is sufficient to show that $tag_{op1} \neq tag_{op2}$. In case the writer invoking $op1$ is not the same as the writer invoking $op2$, this is immediate since

$cid_{op1} \neq cid_{op2}$. On the other hand, if the writer is the same, assume without loss of generality that $op1$ precedes $op2$ in H_{ex} (this assumption can be made since executions are assumed to be well-formed). Then, it is not difficult to see that, by the non-empty quorum intersection between quorum Q_w accessed in Write phase of $op1$ and Q_r accessed in the Timestamp synchronization phase of $op2$, we have $maxts \geq ts_{op1}$ in $op2$. Since $ts_{op2} = maxts + 1$, we have $ts_{op1} < ts_{op2}$, i.e., $op1 \prec op2$. □

Remark 4.3 The generalized ABD algorithm remains correct when an arbitrary quorum system $\boldsymbol{QS}$ underlies the implementation instead of an asymmetric read-write quorum $\boldsymbol{AQS}$. In this case, in each phase, the clients simply act upon reception of $readack/writeack$ messages from any quorum in $\boldsymbol{QS}$. Wait freedom is guaranteed as long as $\exists Q \in \boldsymbol{QS}$ such that $Q \subseteq alive(S)$.

4.2 CONSENSUS EMULATION

Quorum intersections are fundamental to the solutions to consensus problem as well. In this section, we explain how the consensus algorithm (called Synod) from the celebrated Paxos state-machine replication protocol [Lamport, 1998, 2001] employs quorums to achieve the highest possible level of consistency in distributed systems [Boichat et al., 2003].

We focus on Paxos/Synod safety properties, namely Validity and, in particular, Agreement. Furthermore, we assume the asynchronous message passing crash-fault model, and an eventual leader failure detector Ω, as defined in Sec. 2.5 that helps ensure Termination. The Ω failure detector applies to the set of $proposers$. We assume $\mathcal{P}$ different proposers taking IDs from a set $1 \ldots \mathcal{P}$. We also assume a quorum system $\boldsymbol{QS}$ over a set of $acceptors$ satisfying the invariant $\exists Q \in \boldsymbol{QS} : Q \subseteq alive(acceptors)$.

4.2.1 SYNOD TERMINATION

Synod relies on Ω for liveness, but also on the variant of consensus, that is not subject to the FLP impossibility result [Fischer et al., 1985]. We call this variant *Obstruction-free* consensus, or simply OFC. Like consensus, OFC may return a learned value to a learner, but, unlike consensus OFC can return a special *abort* signal to the proposer. Moreover, in OFC a proposer can propose a value more than once (unlike in consensus). OFC has the same properties as consensus, except that the termination is replaced with *obstruction-free (OF) termination*.

- (OF Termination) If a correct proposer p proposes a value, then eventually, every correct learner learns a value or p aborts. Moreover, if a single correct proposer p proposes a value infinitely many times, then p does not abort forever.

With OFC and Ω consensus is very simple to implement. The proposers' code for Synod protocol using OFC and Ω is given in Algorithm 5.

Algorithm 5 Synod implementation using SynodOFC and Ω

code of proposer p

Local variables initialization: $val \leftarrow \perp; decision \leftarrow abort$

---

upon $inv_p(Synod, propose(v))$ **do**
  periodically $send(propose, v)$ to $leader()$
end upon
upon $receive\ (propose, v)$ from some proposer **do**
  $val \leftarrow v$
  loop
    if $p = leader()$ and $decision = abort$ **then**
      $decision \leftarrow inv_p(OFC, propose(val))$
    end if
  end loop
end upon

---

code of learner l

---

upon $resp_l(SynodOFC, learn, v)$ **do**
  return $resp_l(Synod, learn, v)$
end upon

It is indeed straightforward to see that the properties of Ω and OFC guarantee Synod Termination. Indeed, denote by l the eventual stable leader output by Ω. By properties of Ω, l is correct. Since a correct proposer proposes a value it will eventually send a $propose$ message to l. Then, l will be the only proposer to propose infinitely many times a value to OFC, and the Synod Termination follows from OF Termination.

Since OFC has the same Validity and Agreement properties as consensus, these properties are inherited by Synod from OFC. In the following, we give a *SynodOFC* implementation of OFC contained within the original Synod algorithm [Lamport, 1998, 2001]. At the heart of the implementation is the classical notion of quorum systems.

4.2.2 QUORUM-BASED SYNODOFC

SynodOFC is given in Algorithms 6 and 7. On the very high level, the SynodOFC implementation resembles that of a $write$ operation of the generalized ABD described earlier.

Namely, the SynodOFC implementation consists of 2 phases, simply called *Phase 1* and *Phase 2*. Resembling to a combination of the Timestamp synchronization phase of the $write$ operation and the read phase in the *read* operation in ABD, Phase 1 is there to ensure consistency in presence of multiple proposers proposing values to SynodOFC (cf. concurrent writers in ABD). Only in the Phase 2 are some messages propagated to learners, corresponding roughly to the Write phase of the ABD *write* operation.

Algorithm 6 SynodOFC implementation (pseudocode of proposer p)

Local variables initialization: $ballot_p \leftarrow p - \mathcal{P}$; $val \leftarrow \bot$

1: **upon** $inv_p(SynodOFC, propose(v))$ **do**
2:     $ballot_p \leftarrow ballot_p + \mathcal{P}$
3:     **Phase 1:**
4:        $send(p1, ballot_p)$ to all acceptors
5:        **when** $receive$ $(p1ack, ballot_p, bal_i, val_i)$ **or** $(p1abort, ballot_p)$
          from all a_i from some $Q \in \mathbf{QS}$
6:           **if** received some $p1abort$ **then**
7:              **return** $resp_p(SynodOFC, abort)$
8:           **end if**
9:           **leaderSelect**(received $p1ack$ messages, val, v)
10:       **end when**
11:    **Phase 2:**
12:       $send(p2, ballot_p, val)$ to all acceptors
13:       **when** $receive$ $(p2abort, ballot_p)$
14:          **return** $resp_p(SynodOFC, abort)$
15:       **end when**
16: **end upon**
17: **procedure leaderSelect**($msgs, val, v$)
18:    $maxbal \leftarrow$ maximum $m.bal_i$ for all $m \in msgs$
19:    $maxval \leftarrow m.val_i$ for $m \in msgs$ with $m.bal_i = maxbal$
20:    **if** $maxval \neq \bot$ **then**
21:       $val \leftarrow maxval$
22:    **else**
23:       $val \leftarrow v$
24:    **end if**
25: **end procedure**

In the SynodOFC protocol, the fundamental notion is that of a *ballot*. Ballots act like timestamps and their role is to totally order proposals coming from different proposers. On proposing

Algorithm 7 SynodOFC implementation (acceptors and learners pseudocode)

code of acceptor a

Local variables initialization: $p1ballot \leftarrow 0$; $p2ballot \leftarrow 0$; $val \leftarrow \bot$

```
upon receive (p1, ballot) from some proposer p do
    if p1ballot ≥ ballot or p2ballot ≥ ballot then
        send(p1abort, ballot) to p
    else
        p1ballot ← ballot
        send(p1ack, ballot, p2bal, val) to p
    end if
end upon
upon receive (p2, ballot, v) from some proposer p do
    if p1ballot > ballot or p2ballot > ballot then
        send(p2abort, ballot) to p
    else
        val ← v; p2ballot ← ballot
        send(p2ack, ballot, v) to all learners
    end if
end upon
```

code of learner l

```
upon receive (p2ack, ballot, v) from all a_i from some Q ∈ QS do
    return resp_l(SynodOFC, learn, v)
end upon
```

a value to SynodOFC, a proposer increments its ballot number $ballot_p$ by $\mathcal{P}$, the total number of proposers. Ballots are initialized such that the ballot number of the first proposal of proposer p is p.

In the Phase 1, proposer p sends a $p1ack$ message telling acceptors not to accept any other proposal with a ballot number less or equal to $ballot_p$. If an acceptor already promised not to accept $ballot_p$ (by replying to a $p1$ message with a higher ballot number), an acceptor sends a $p1abort$ message to p. Otherwise, an acceptors informs the acceptor of a value it has previously accepted and the corresponding ballot number using a $p1ack$ message.

The critical point in Phase 1 is when the proposer receives $p1ack$ or $p1abort$ messages from a quorum of acceptors. If any acceptor replied with $p1abort$, the proposer simply returns $abort$. In the other case, if all messages from a quorum of acceptors, are $p1ack$ messages, the proposer adopts the proposal value with the highest ballot number in the received quorum, if any (see lines 9, and 17-25 in Algorithm 6). As we will see shortly this guarantees that if some learned a proposal v with a given ballot number b, the acceptors can only accept v in later ballots higher than b.

In Phase 2, proposer p disseminates its proposal value v to acceptors, still under ballot number $ballot_p$, by sending a $p2$ message. Unless some other proposer started Phase 1 with a higher ballot number in the meantime, a quorum of acceptors will *accept* value v. Alternatively, if some proposer already started a ballot with a higher number, an acceptor might send a $p2abort$ message to the proposer, causing the proposer to return $abort$.

On accepting v, acceptor a stores v locally and sends a $p2ack$ message containing ballot number $ballot_p$ and accepted value v to all learners. Finally, a learner learns a value, if it receives $p2ack$ messages from a quorum of acceptors with the same value and the same ballot number.

4.2.2.1 Correctness arguments

It is straightforward to show that SynodOFC maintains consensus Validity. OF Termination is slightly less obvious, yet still not difficult to prove by assuming a single proposer that keeps proposing to SynodOFC with increasingly higher ballot numbers. In the following, we focus on arguments based on quorum intersections, critical to proving Agreement.

Definition 4.4 If some learner learns value v by receiving a quorum of $(p2ack, ballot, v)$ messages, we say that a learner learns v in $ballot$.

Definition 4.5 If a quorum of acceptors accepts v by receiving $(p2, ballot, v)$ messages, we say that v is *chosen* in $ballot$.

The proof of the following Lemma is straightforward.

Lemma 4.6 *If a learner learns v in ballot b, then v is chosen in b.*

The following Lemma with the proof based on quorum intersections, is crucial to show Agreement.

Lemma 4.7 *If a value v is chosen in b, then an acceptor can only accept v in ballots higher than b.*

Proof. *(Sketch)* The proof follows directly from the non-empty intersection property of quorums. By Definition 4.5 a quorum Q of acceptors accepted v by receiving the $(p2, b, v)$ message.

Assume by contradiction, that some acceptor accepts $v' \neq v$ in a ballot $b' > b$ and let b' be the lowest ballot number in which this occurs. This can only happen if some proposer p starts the Phase 2 with a ballot number $b' > b$, which implies that p already completed Phase 1, with ballot number b'. This in turn implies that p received $(p1ack, b', *, *)$ messages from a quorum Q' of acceptors. Denote by $t_{end\,P1,b'}$ the time when this occurs. Furthermore, denote by $t_{accept,v,b}$ the time when the last acceptor a from $Q \cap Q'$ receives a $(p2, b, v)$ message.

We distinguish two cases:

1. $t_{end\,P1,b'} > t_{accept,v,b}$, in this case, p adopts v in b' and hence, $v' = v$. A contradiction; and

2. $t_{end\,P1,b'} < t_{accept,v,b}$. In this case, acceptor a already sent a $p1ack$ message in ballot b' before receiving $(p2, b, v)$. Hence, on receiving $(p2, b, v)$, a cannot accept v. A contradiction.

□

With Lemma 4.7 proved, it is immediate to see that no two different values can be learned in different ballot numbers. Learning different values in the same ballot number is also not possible, since a proposer and acceptors never send different values with the same ballot number. The Agreement follows.

4.3 DYNAMIC STORAGE EMULATION

The ABD storage algorithm and the Synod consensus algorithm assume static process membership. In many applications the context is *dynamic*, in the sense that processes continuously join and leave the system. In such a dynamic context, quorums might change all the time and, hence, need to be *reconfigured*. In this section we will discuss the RAMBO protocol [Gilbert et al., 2010], an atomic storage algorithm specifically designed for the dynamic context. RAMBO is an asynchronous message-passing protocol, tolerating crash faults of the participating processes. Each RAMBO process comes from (a possibly infinite) universe U, with a unique identifier, where the identifiers are totally ordered. RAMBO does not distinguish client and server roles; in ABD parlance (Sec. 4.1), each RAMBO process is both a client and a server.

On a high level, RAMBO utilizes and combines the techniques of ABD and Synod. More specifically, RAMBO consists of three basic components at each process:

- The $Joiner$ component dedicated to bootstrapping a process to the RAMBO protocol. The $Joiner$ component of a given process tries to contact the processes it suspects to be already part of RAMBO in order to join the protocol. On the other hand, a process that leaves the RAMBO protocol is simply assumed to be crashed.

- The $Recon$ component is dedicated to reconfiguring quorums as nodes join and leave. It is based on a generic consensus algorithm, so using Synod consensus algorithm fits perfectly. In the Synod parlance, every RAMBO process acts in all three roles: as a proposer, acceptor and learner. $Recon$ asynchronously installs new quorum configurations when requested by RAMBO client. As new configurations are installed, old ones become obsolete, yet $Recon$ does not garbage collect old configurations — this task is left to the third component.

- The $Reader - Writer$ component (or, simply RWC) is a variant of the generalized ABD protocol. In fact, if quorum reconfigurations never occur, RAMBO and RWC precisely boil down to the ABD protocol. In the ABD parlance, every RAMBO process acts as a both client and a server. Not surprisingly, the RWC component is at the heart of RAMBO and its main goal is to preserve atomicity in the presence of changing quorum configurations. In addition, RWC also garbage collects old configurations, since the subprotocol used for this purpose is itself a variant of the RWC $read$ and $write$ operation implementations.

The key notion in RAMBO is that of a *configuration*. A configuration c is a record containing the information about a specific set of read and write quorums: (1) $c.rq$ is a set system which represents read quorums; and (2) $c.wq$ is a set system which represents write quorums of configuration c. The union $c.rq \cup c.wq$ is an asymmetric read/write quorum system according to Definition 3.10. We denote the set of all possible such configurations by C.

There are two exceptions in the form of special configuration values that are relevant to RAMBO, but that do not belong to C. These configurations are denoted by: (1) $\perp$, to designate a configuration that is not known to a process; and (2) $\pm$, to designate a garbage collected configuration.

Notation 4.8 We denote by $members(c)$ the set of all RAMBO processes in a given configuration $c \in C$. More formally:

$$members(c) \stackrel{\text{def}}{=} \{q \in U | \exists RQ \in c.rq, \exists WQ \in c.wq : q \in RQ \vee q \in WQ\}.$$

Each RAMBO process p maintains the state containing several variables, out of which the most important ones are the following.

- The $world_p$ variable is a set of all identifiers of all processes known to p. Process p adds process q to $world_p$ as soon as it receives any protocol message from q. In RAMBO, $world_p$ is a monotonic variable, i.e., a process identifier is never removed from $world_p$.

- The $cmap_p$ variable is a configuration map, i.e., an array of configurations. Each element $cmap_p[k]$ holds information about a given configuration c with configuration number k. For simplicity, in the context of $cmap_*$, we sometimes refer to "configuration k" when we should be referring to "configuration number k". If $c = cmap_p[k] \in C$ we refer to c as to an *active* configuration. As we will see, RAMBO maintains the following fundamental invariant which stipulates that an active configuration k is the same at all processes:

$$\forall p, q \in U, \forall k \in \mathbb{N}_0 : (cmap_p[k] \in C) \wedge (cmap_q[k] \in C) \Rightarrow cmap_p[k] = cmap_q[k].$$

  Additionally, $cmap_p$ contains information about the special inactive configurations as well: (1) $cmap_p[k] = \perp$, if configuration k is not known to process p, and (2) $cmap_p[k] = \pm$, if configuration k has been garbage collected at process p. RAMBO garbage collection procedure ensures that if $cmap_p[k] = \pm$, then $cmap_p[j] = \pm$, for all $j < k$.

Besides $world_p$ and $cmap_p$, process p maintains several other variables that we describe later. For clarity, we introduce the following notation.

Notation 4.9 If a component X maintains variable var that is modified *only* in communication with another local component Y, we denote var by var^Y.

In the following, we describe all three components of the RAMBO protocol. We first describe the two main RAMBO components, namely $Recon$ and RWC and then we describe the $Joiner$ component.

4.3.1 THE *Recon* COMPONENT

The main pseudocode of $Recon$, responsible for quorum reconfiguration, is given in Algorithm 8. We postpone the code for communication with other local components (i.e., $Joiner$ and RWC) to Algorithm 13.

As we already mentioned, $Recon$ relies on the consensus (e.g., Synod) protocol to install new configurations. To this end $Recon$ maintains the additional configuration map rec_cmap_p which holds information about configuration that a consensus is reached upon. Unlike the main $cmap_p$, p never garbage collects rec_cmap_p.

$Recon$ receives requests for reconfiguration externally, from a RAMBO client. The reconfiguration request is of form $recon(c, c')$, where c is the current configuration and the c' is the configuration that the client proposes. The choice of read and write quorums proposed for the new configuration c' is out of scope; in practice, this choice might depend on the application. We assume that RAMBO is externally initialized with the initial configuration c_{init} under configuration number 0.

The reconfiguration code is relatively straightforward. Upon receiving $recon(c, c')$ request (line 1, Algorithm 8), $Recon$ selects the highest known configuration number k in rec_cmap_p (line 2, Algorithm 8). If the old configuration c matches $rec\_cmap_p[k]$ (line 3, Algorithm 8), $Recon$ bootstraps configuration $k+1$ by putting c' in $cprop_p[k+1]$ (line 4, Algorithm 8). The array $cprop_p$ holds configuration proposal values to be used in consensus.

In order to install a new configuration $k+1$, $Recon$ first waits for a confirmation that a preceding configuration k has been successfully installed by RWC component (line 8, Algorithm 8). Then, $Recon$ runs a consensus service among elements of $members(c)$, where c is the old reconfiguration equal to $rec\_cmap_p[k]$.

Notation 4.10 We denote $propose$ (resp., $learn$) events in at process p, in a consensus instance k, executed among processes from set S by $propose_{p,k,S}$ (resp., $learn_{p,k,S}$).

Algorithm 8 The main pseudocode of the *Recon* component

Local variables initialization:

$rec\_cmap_p \leftarrow \langle c_{init}, \bot, \bot, \ldots \rangle$
$cprop_p \leftarrow \langle \bot, \bot, \ldots \rangle$
$installed_p^{RWC} \leftarrow \{0\}$
$pending_p \leftarrow \emptyset$
$proposed_p \leftarrow \emptyset$

1: **upon** $receive\ recon(c, c')$ request from RAMBO client **do**
2: $\quad k \leftarrow$ select maximum k' such that $rec\_cmap_p[k'] \in C$
3: $\quad$ **if** $c = rec\_cmap_p[k]$ and $cprop_p[k+1] = \bot$ **then**
4: $\quad\quad cprop_p[k+1] = c'$
5: $\quad\quad pending_p \leftarrow pending_p \cup \{k+1\}$
6: $\quad$ **end if**
7: **end upon**
8: **upon** $cprop_p[k+1] \neq \bot$ **and** $k+1 \notin proposed_p$ **and** $k \in installed_p^{RWC}$ **do**
9: $\quad propose_{p,k+1,members(rec\_cmap[k])}(cprop_p[k+1])$
10: $\quad proposed_p \leftarrow proposed_p \cup \{k+1\}$
11: **end upon**
12: **upon** $learn_{p,k,c}(c'')$ **do**
13: $\quad rec\_cmap_p[k] \leftarrow c''$
14: **end upon**
15: **upon** $rec\_cmap_p[k] \in C$ **and** $k \in pending_p$ **do**
16: $\quad pending_p \leftarrow pending_p \setminus \{k\}$
17: $\quad$ **return** $recon\_ack(rec\_cmap_p[k])$ to RAMBO client
18: **end upon**

Upon learning a value in consensus instance $k+1$, *Recon* populates $rec\_cmap_p[k+1]$ with the learned value which might differ from the proposed configuration c' (lines 12-14, Algorithm 8) and informs the client of the new configuration using $recon\_ack$ (lines 15-18, Algorithm 8).

Remark 4.11 In the original RAMBO algorithm [Gilbert et al., 2010], *Recon* components periodically gossip the consensus values they proposed (i.e., $cprop_p[k+1]$) and learned (i.e., $rec\_cmap_p[k+1]$) among members of the old configuration, $members(c)$. For simplicity and clarity, these gossip messages are not explicitly shown in Algorithm 8.

Remark 4.12 All the **upon** clauses in Algorithm 8 are additionally conditional upon boolean $active_p^{Joiner}$ that we discuss in Sec. 4.3.3.

4.3.2 THE *RWC* COMPONENT

The *RWC* component exports two operations to the RAMBO client: $write(v)$ and $read()$. Conceptually, RAMBO *read* and *write* operations is very similar to those of ABD. Each process p stores a local copy of the shared variable val_p as well as $tag_p = \langle ts, ID\rangle$ which contains the highest timestamp of the shared variable and the identifier of the RAMBO process that issued the *write*. Moreover, each operation consists of two phases, in which a RAMBO process first reads some information from read quorums (like the Timestamp synchronization phase of ABD *write* and the read phase of ABD *read*) and then writes some information to write quorums (like the Write phase of ABD *write* and the Writeback phase of ABD *read*). In RAMBO, the first phase of an operation is called the *query* phase, whereas the second phase of an operation is called the *propagate* phase.

The key differences between *read* and *write* operations in RAMBO and ABD are the following:

- In RAMBO, in the query (resp., propagate) phase a process p waits for a read (resp., write) quorum from *all* known, non garbage collected configurations. In a sense, RAMBO executes the ABD protocol on all active configurations simultaneously.
- In RAMBO, processes do not only reply to the process that invoked the operation, but rather continuously gossip messages that correspond to ABD *readack* and *writeack* messages to all the processes in the local $world_p$.

In fact, RAMBO unifies different message types used in ABD into a single message *rambo*, which exchanges all the relevant information among RAMBO processes. More specifically, a *rambo* message sent from process p to process q has the following format:

$$(rambo, val_p, tag_p, world_p, cmap_p, phaseCnt_p, phase_p[q])$$

Hence, to a message containing the information about the latest val_p and tag_p, process p piggybacks the information about the local $world_p$ and $cmap_p$. This allows processes to exchange more efficiently the information about participating processes and known configurations. Finally, a *rambo* message includes the counters that define the freshness of the information: $phaseCnt_p$ which is incremented once per every phase of every operation at the sender p, and $phase_p[q]$ the last phase number of the receiver q known to sender p.

We are now ready to describe RAMBO *read* and *write* operations. We first explain the pseudocode given in Algorithm 9 and then pay special attention to the code for processing *rambo* messages which we give separately in Algorithm 10.

The state of each operation invoked by process p is captured by the op_p record, containing the information about the *type* of the operation (*read* or *write*), operation *phase* (*idle*, *query* or

---

Algorithm 9 The RWC component: $read$ and $write$ operations

Local variables initialization:

   $phaseCnt_p \leftarrow 0;\ phase_p \leftarrow \langle 0, 0 \ldots \rangle;\ val_p \leftarrow \bot;\ tag_p.[ts, id] \leftarrow \langle 0, 0 \rangle;\ world_p \leftarrow \emptyset;$
   $state_p \leftarrow idle; cmap_p \leftarrow \langle c_{init}, \bot, \bot, \ldots \rangle$
   $op_p.[type, phase, phaseCnt, val, ack, cmap] \leftarrow \langle read, idle, 0, \bot, \emptyset, \langle \bot, \bot, \ldots \rangle \rangle$

1: **upon** $receive\ write(v)$ request from RAMBO client **and** $state_p \neq idle$ **do**
2:    $phaseCnt_p \leftarrow phaseCnt_p + 1$
3:    $op_p.[type, phase, phaseCnt, val, ack, cmap] \leftarrow \langle write, query, phaseCnt_p, v, \emptyset, cmap_p \rangle$
4: **end upon**

5: **upon** $receive\ read()$ request from RAMBO client **and** $state_p \neq idle$ **do**
6:    $phaseCnt_p \leftarrow phaseCnt_p + 1$
7:    $op_p.[type, phase, phaseCnt, val, ack, cmap] \leftarrow \langle read, query, phaseCnt_p, \bot, \emptyset, cmap_p \rangle$
8: **end upon**

9: **upon** $op_p.phase = query$ **and** $state_p = active$ **and**
        $\forall k \in \mathbb{N}_0 : op_p.cmap[k] \in C \Rightarrow \exists RQ \in op_p.cmap[k].rq : RQ \subseteq op_p.ack$ **do**
10:    **if** $op_p.type = read$ **then**
11:      $op_p.val = val_p$
12:    **else**
13:      $tag_p \leftarrow \langle tag_p.ts + 1, p \rangle$
14:      $val_p \leftarrow op_p.val$
15:    **end if**
16:    $phaseCnt_p \leftarrow phaseCnt_p + 1$
17:    $op_p.[phase, phaseCnt, ack, cmap] \leftarrow \langle propagate, phaseCnt_p, \emptyset, cmap_p \rangle$
18: **end upon**

19: **upon** $op_p.phase = propagate$ **and** $state_p = active$ **and**
        $\forall k \in \mathbb{N}_0 : op_p.cmap[k] \in C \Rightarrow \exists WQ \in op_p.cmap[k].wq : WQ \subseteq op_p.ack$ **do**
20:    $op_p.phase \leftarrow idle$
21:    **if** $op_p.type = read$ **then**
22:      **return** $op_p.val$
23:    **else**
24:      **return** ack
25:    **end if**
26: **end upon**

27: **upon** $state_p = active$ **do**
28:    $q \leftarrow$ select element from $world_p$ with uniform probability
29:    $send(rambo, val_p, tag_p, world_p, cmap_p, phaseCnt_p, phase_p[q])$ to q
30: **end upon**

---

propagate) and phase number *phaseCnt*, value *val* to be returned (resp., written) in the case of *read* (resp., *write*), set *ack* which contains the IDs of processes that replied in the current phase and *cmap*, a configuration map holding active configurations that the operation must access. Upon invocation of a *read* or *write* operation, *RCW* simply increments the phase counter $phaseCnt_p$ and bootstraps the record op_p (lines 1-8, Algorithm 9). Notably, operation phase counter $op_p.phaseCnt$ takes the value of the phase counter $phaseCnt_p$, $op_p.cmap$ is set to the last known $cmap_p$, and operation phase $op_p.phase$ is set to *query*.

In both query and propagate phase of an operation, a process collects *rambo* messages that processes asynchronously gossip (lines 27-30, Algorithm 9). The query phase completes once process p receives replies from at least one read quorum in *every* active configuration in $op_p.cmap$ (line 9, Algorithm 9). Roughly speaking, this guarantees that p will learn about the latest value (or tag) written, regardless of the configuration(s) in which the value was written. As we will shortly see (Algorithm 10), as p receives *rambo* messages from other processes, it continuously updates its local copy with the latest tag_p and value val_p.

Therefore, upon completion of the query phase, the process possesses locally the latest tag and value read from at least one read quorum of every configuration in $op_p.cmap$. Hence, in the case of *read* operation, p locally selects val_p as the value to be returned ($op_p.val$, line 11, Algorithm 9), whereas in the case *write* operation, p increments the timestamp portion of the tag and writes the new value locally in val_p (lines 13-14, Algorithm 9). This faithfully corresponds to the client code executed in ABD upon the end of the first phase. Finally, p bootstraps the propagate phase, notably by incrementing the phase counters and putting a fresh copy of $cmap_p$ into $op_p.cmap$ (lines 16-17, Algorithm 9).

Analogously to the query phase, the propagate phase completes once p receives replies from at least one write quorum from every active configuration in $op_p.cmap$ (lines 19-26, Algorithm 9).

So far, our description of *RWC* strongly resembles to that of ABD run on multiple quorum configurations simultaneously. However, *RWC* bears additional complexity, related to processing the gossiped information about quorum configurations. To clarify this, we turn to Algorithm 10, and explain how *rambo* messages are processed.

When p receives $m = (rambo, v, tag, world, cm, qPhase, pPhase)$ message from some process q, it first enlarges its local knowledge of participating processes $world_p$ with *world* as perceived by q (line 3, Algorithm 10) and updates the local phase counter of process q if needed (line 5, Algorithm 10). This will be subsequently used by q (upon receiving messages sent later by p to q) to know that p received m. Then, if m bears information about a more recent value and tag, p updates val_p and tag_p, as we already mentioned (lines 7-9, Algorithm 10).

Gossiping *rambo* messages also serves to disseminate information about new and garbage collected configurations. To merge this gossiped information with local configuration maps, *RWC* uses two simple and intuitive procedures: (1) **newUpdate**(cm_1, cm_2) (lines 24-28, Algorithm 10), which extends cm_1 with the information about configurations from cm_2 that were not known by cm_1; and (2) **gcUpdate**(cm_1, cm_2); (lines 29-33, Algorithm 10), which updates cm_1 with the

Algorithm 10 The RWC component: processing $rambo$ messages

1: **upon** $receive\,(rambo, v, tag, world, cm, qPhase, pPhase)$ from q **and** $state_p \neq idle$ **do**
2:     $state_p \leftarrow active$
3:     $world_p \leftarrow world_p \cup world$
4:     **if** $phase_p[q] < qPhase$ **then**
5:        $phase_p[q] \leftarrow qPhase$
6:     **end if**
7:     **if** $tag.ts > tag_p.ts$ **or** $(tag.ts = tag_p.ts$ **and** $tag.id > tag_p.id)$ **then**
8:        $val_p \leftarrow v; tag_p \leftarrow tag$
9:     **end if**
10:    **newUpdate**$(cmap_p, cm)$
11:    **gcUpdate**$(cmap_p, cm)$
12:    **if** $op_p.phase \neq idle$ **and** $pPhase \geq op_p.phaseCnt$ **then**
13:       **newUpdate**$(op_p.cmap, cm)$
14:       **if** **usable**$(op_p.cmap)$ **then**
15:          $op_p.ack \leftarrow op_p.ack \cup \{q\}$
16:       **else**   *{Restart current operation phase}*
17:          $phaseCnt_p \leftarrow phaseCnt_p + 1$
18:          $op_p.[phaseCnt, ack, cmap] \leftarrow \langle phaseCnt_p, \emptyset, cmap_p \rangle$
19:       **end if**
20:    **else**
21:       **gcprocess**()   *{see Algorithm 12}*
22:    **end if**
23: **end upon**

24: **procedure newUpdate**(cm_1, cm_2) *{Updates cm_1 with previously unknown configurations}*
25:    **for** $k \in \{k' \in \mathbb{N}_0 | cm_1[k'] = \bot \wedge cm_2[k'] \neq \bot\}$ **do**
26:       $cm_1[k] \leftarrow cm_2[k]$
27:    **end for**
28: **end procedure**

29: **procedure gcUpdate**(cm_1, cm_2) *{Updates cm_1 with information about gc-ed configurations}*
30:    **for** $k \in \{k' \in \mathbb{N}_0 | cm_2[k'] = \pm\}$ **do**
31:       $cm_1[k] \leftarrow cm_2[k]$
32:    **end for**
33: **end procedure**

34: **function usable**(cm)
35:    **return** $\forall k, k', k'' \in \mathbb{N}_0 : cm[k], cm[k''] \in C \wedge k < k' < k'' \Rightarrow cm[k'] \in C$
36: **end function**

information on garbage collected configurations from cm_2. With every *rambo* message received, p applies the mentioned procedures to local $cmap_p$, using the incoming configuration map cm (lines 10-11, Algorithm 10). Hence, the following *read* and *write* operations will work only with quorums from most recent active configurations known to p. However, this is not exactly true for a possibly pending operation at p as we will shortly see.

Namely, if there is a *read* or *write* operation pending at p, and if message m is sent by q in response to the current operation phase (line 12, Algorithm 10), p must first update the configuration map of the pending operation $op_p.cmap$ with the information about new configurations from cm (using the **newUpdate** procedure, line 13, Algorithm 10). Clearly, the pending operation must take into account newly discovered configurations as well and access their quorums as well. Otherwise, some other process r might have already completed written a value into a new configuration which might lead to violating consistency.

However, $op_p.cmap$ cannot simply take the value of $cmap_p$ which, by this point, also includes the information about garbage collected configurations from cm. Namely, the pending operation must continue to access quorums from old configurations as well.

Then, after updating $op_p.cmap$ with newly discovered configurations, p checks whether the resulting $op_p.cmap$ is *usable* (lines 34-36, Algorithm 10); in short, a configuration map is usable if its subsequence of active configurations is gapless, i.e., if there are no garbage collected configurations in between two active configuration numbers.

If $op_p.cmap$ is usable, q is added to $op_p.ack$, i.e., m is treated as the acknowledgement that the pending operation by p accessed q (line 15, Algorithm 10). On the other hand, if $op_p.cmap$ is not usable, which indicates that reconfigurations are occurring frequently, the current operation phase must be restarted (line 16-18, Algorithm 10) with $op_p.cmap$ equal to the latest configuration map $cmap_p$.

Remark 4.13 It is not difficult to prove the invariant that $cmap_p$ is always usable. Namely, while the **newUpdate** procedure might render the configuration unusable, this is rectified by the application of the **gcUpdate** procedure (lines 10-11, Algorithm 10).

Finally, if there is no pending operation ongoing, *rambo* might influence the garbage collection procedure (line 21, Algorithm 10), as discussed in the following.

However, before describing the garbage collection part of RWC we explain how new configurations are transferred from the $Recon$ component to the RWC component.

4.3.2.1 Configuration installation

Configuration installation is rather straightforward; the pseudocode for both $Recon$ and RWC component is given in Algorithm 11. Once GWC is active (i.e., when $state_p = active$), and all configurations with numbers smaller than k are known to p, i.e., for all $j < k$ $cmap_p \in C \cup \{\pm\}$, the RWC requests new configuration from $Recon$.

Algorithm 11 Installation of new configurations: code of RWC and $Recon$ at process p

RWC code

upon $status_p = active$ **and** $\exists k \in \mathbb{N}, \forall j < k : cmap_p[j] \neq \bot \wedge cmap_p[k] = \bot$ **do**
  invoke $request\_config(k)$ on local $Recon$
end upon

upon $install\_config(k, c)$ response from local $Recon$ **do**
  if $cmap_p[k] \neq \pm$ **then**
    $cmap_p[k] \leftarrow c$
  end if
  newUpdate$(op_p.cmap, cmap_p)$
end upon

$Recon$ code

Local variables initialization: $installRequests_p^{RWC} \leftarrow \emptyset$

---

upon $request\_config(k)$ invocation from RWC **and** $active_p^{Joiner}$ **do**
  $installRequests_p^{RWC} \leftarrow installRequests^{RWC} \cup \{k\}$
end upon

upon $\exists k \in \mathbb{N} : rec\_cmap_p[k] \in C \wedge k \in installRequests_p^{RWC} \wedge k \notin installed_p^{RWC}$ **do**
  $installed_p^{RWC} \leftarrow installed_p^{RWC} \cup \{k\}$
  return $install\_config(k, rec\_cmap_p[k])$ to local RWC
end upon

Then, $Recon$ puts the requested configuration number k in $installRequests_p^{RWC}$ and responds to RWC with $install\_config(k, rec\_cmap_p[k])$ once it learns the value in the respective consensus instance.

Finally, RWC processes the $install\_config(k, c)$ response by storing c in $cmap_p[k]$ (unless configuration k has already been garbage collected) and updates the configuration map of a possibly pending operation $op_p.cmap$.

4.3.2.2 Garbage collection

The reason configurations are garbage collected within the RWC component rather than in the $Recon$ component is that the garbage collection (GC) procedure is only a slight variation of the *read* and *write* operations. Like *read* and *write* operations, the GC procedure relies on the *rambo* message gossip. Moreover, garbage collection ensures the critical aspect of RAMBO: namely, consistency across different configurations, so its naturally belongs to RWC.

Garbage collection code is given in Algorithm 12. The state of the GC procedure at process p is captured by the record gc_p, very similar to the op_p record, with a new field $gc_p.config$ that holds the highest configuration number k. GC garbage collects all configurations with numbers smaller than $gc_p.config$.

Algorithm 12 The RWC component: garbage collection

Local variables initialization:

$gc_p.[config, phase, phaseCnt, ack, cmap] \leftarrow \langle 0, idle, 0, \emptyset, \langle \bot, \bot, \ldots \rangle \rangle$

1: **upon** $gc_p.phase = idle$ **and** $state_p \neq idle$ **and**
  $\exists k \in \mathbb{N}, \forall j < k : cmap[k] \in C \wedge cmap[k-1] \in C \wedge cmap[j] \neq \bot$ **do**
2: $phaseCnt_p \leftarrow phaseCnt_p + 1$
3: $gc_p.[config, phase, phaseCnt, ack, cmap] \leftarrow \langle k, query, phaseCnt_p, \emptyset, cmap_p \rangle$
4: **end upon**

5: **upon** $gc_p.phase = query$ **and** $gc_p.config = k$ **and** $state_p = active$ **and**
  $\forall j < k : gc_p.cmap[j] \in C \Rightarrow \exists RQ \in gc_p.cmap[j].rq : RQ \subseteq gc_p.ack$ **and**
  $\forall j < k : gc_p.cmap[j] \in C \Rightarrow \exists WQ \in gc_p.cmap[j].wq : WQ \subseteq gc_p.ack$ **do**
6: $phaseCnt_p \leftarrow phaseCnt_p + 1$
7: $gc_p.[phase, phaseCnt, ack] \leftarrow \langle propagate, phaseCnt_p, \emptyset \rangle$
8: **end upon**

9: **upon** $gc_p.phase = propagate$ **and** $gc_p.config = k$ **and** $state_p = active$ **and**
  $\exists WQ \in gc_p.cmap[k].wq : WQ \subseteq gc_p.ack$ **do**
10: **for** $j = 1$ to $k - 1$ **do**
11:   $cmap_p \leftarrow \pm$
12: **end for**
13: $gc_p.phase \leftarrow idle$
14: **end upon**

15: **procedure gcprocess()** *{Part of Algorithm 10, line 21, upon reception of $rambo$ message}*
16: **if** $gc_p.phase \neq idle$ **and** $pPhase \geq gc_p.phaseCnt$ **then**
17:   $gc_p.ack \leftarrow gc_p.ack \cup \{q\}$
18: **end if**
19: **end procedure**

The garbage collection procedure is invoked once there exists a configuration k and an older, still active configuration $k - 1$ in $cmap_p$ (line 1, Algorithm 12). Just like $read$ and $write$, the GC procedure has two phases: query and propagate.

The query phase completes once *rambo* messages are received from at least one read quorum and at least one write quorum from every configuration smaller than k that was active at the beginning of the phase (line 5, Algorithm 12). Accessing read quorums from old configurations is needed so that the RWC component can learn about the latest value and tag in every old configuration before these become garbage collected (recall that tags and values are updated when a *rambo* message is received, Algorithm 10). Along with the propagate phase of the GC procedure, this guarantees that, once old configurations are garbage collected, configuration k will maintain global consistency, by having the tag and value at least as recent as every write that had completed in an old configuration. On the other hand, write quorums from old configurations must be accessed in the query phase of GC, in order to inform processes in write quorums of old configurations about the existence of configuration k (recall that configuration maps are gossiped using *rambo* messages). Hence, a following *read* or *write* operation *op* accessing an old configuration j will learn about k, since the query phase of *op* must access a read quorum of j, which intersects with the write quorum of j, which will result in an update of the configuration map used in *op* to include configuration k.

Finally, in the propagate phase of GC, the procedure makes sure that at least one write quorum from configuration k is accessed (line 9, Algorithm 12). As we already mentioned, this guarantees that configuration k will hold a values and a tag at least as recent as any operation that has accessed the garbage collected configurations but did not access configuration k.

It is important to note that $gc_p.cmap$ does not need to be updated with the information about new configurations throughout the execution of the GC procedure. This is in contrast to updates made to $op_p.cmap$.

4.3.3 THE *Joiner* COMPONENT

The *Joiner* component is relatively simple and does not involve quorums — we present it here for completeness.

The pseudocode of the component is given in Algorithm 13, along with the related transitions in *Recon* and *RWC* components. *Joiner* exports a single operation to RAMBO client, namely $join(J)$, which serves to bootstrap a node to the protocol and which the client must invoked before it can invoke any other operation on RAMBO. The parameter J of *join* designates the hint from the client about processes that already participate in RAMBO.

4.4 BIBLIOGRAPHIC NOTES

- The ABD algorithm was first presented in [Attiya et al., 1995]. The original majority-based simulation along with the survey of the subsequent work were discussed in a recent article [Attiya, 2010].

- The Paxos replication algorithm was first presented in [Lamport, 1998], with a more accessible presentation appearing in [Lamport, 2001]. An early variant of Paxos, called *viewstamped replication*, was presented in [Oki and Liskov, 1988]. A deconstruction of the Paxos algorithm

---

Algorithm 13 The *Joiner* component and the related *Recon* and *RWC* transitions

---

Joiner code

Local variables initialization:

$joined_p.[Joiner, RWC, Recon] \leftarrow \langle no, no, no \rangle; hints_p \leftarrow \emptyset$

1: **upon** *receive join(J)* request from RAMBO client **and** $joined_p[Joiner] = no$ **do**
2:     $joined_p.[Joiner, RWC, Recon] \leftarrow \langle in\_progress, in\_progress, in\_progress \rangle$
3:     $hints_p \leftarrow J$
4:     **invoke** *join()* on local *Recon* and *RWC*
5: **end upon**

6: **upon** *join_ack* response from local $comp \in \{Recon, RWC\}$ **do**
7:     $joined_p[comp] \leftarrow done$
8:     **if** $joined_p.[Joiner, RWC, Recon] = \langle in\_progress, done, done \rangle$ **then**
9:         $joined_p.[Joiner] \leftarrow done$
10:        **return** *join_ack* to RAMBO client
11:    **end if**
12: **end upon**

13: **upon** $joined_p[Joiner] = in\_progress$ **do**
14:     $q \leftarrow$ select element from $hints_p$ with uniform probability
15:     $send(join$ to q
16: **end upon**

Recon code

Local variables initialization: $active_p^{Joiner} = false$

1: **upon** *join()* invocation from *Joiner* **do**
2:     $active_p^{Joiner} = true$
3:     **return** *join_ack* to local *Joiner*
4: **end upon**

RWC code

Local variables initialization: $active_p^{Joiner} = false$

1: **upon** *join()* invocation from *Joiner* **do**
2:     $active_p^{Joiner} = true$
3:     **return** *join_ack* to local *Joiner*
4: **end upon**

---

that employs eventual leader abstraction and abstracts out the consistency aspects of Paxos appears in [Boichat et al., 2003]. This deconstruction was used as the basis for Paxos presentation in this monograph. The original Paxos replication protocol assumes a variant of the crash failure model in which the processes can recover. Since process recoveries in Paxos are not very relevant for our focus on quorums and their intersections, a simpler crash-stop variant is presented in this monograph.

- RAMBO dynamic storage emulation first appeared in [Lynch and Shvartsman, 2002] with the optimized reconfiguration implementation and the journal version appearing in [Gilbert et al., 2003] and [Gilbert et al., 2010], respectively. These papers describe the protocol in the formal I/O Automata (IOA) model [Lynch and Tuttle, 1989]. A short description of the RAMBO protocol for those not familiar with the IOA model, similar to the one given in this monograph, is given in [Albrecht and Saito, 2005].

- [Naor and Wieder, 2005] employs a specific quorum system, based on a dynamic Voronoi diagram to show a scheme that supports dynamic joins and leaves and that allow processes to handover data to other processes before leaving the system.

- Although RAMBO uses consensus to reconfigure quorums, strictly speaking, consensus is not necessary to implement reconfigurable RAMBO-like atomic memory. This has recently been shown in [Aguilera et al., 2011] where a fully asynchronous dynamic storage emulation is given. This completed the evolution of reconfigurable storage emulation from emulations relying on a centralized quorum reconfigurator [Englert and Shvartsman, 2000, Lynch and Shvartsman, 1997] which offer no fault-tolerance for the reconfiguration mechanism, through the decentralized consensus-based RAMBO reconfiguration [Gilbert et al., 2010] subject to the FLP impossibility result [Fischer et al., 1985], to the fully decentralized, asynchronous and reconfigurable quorum-based storage emulation.

CHAPTER 5

Byzantine Quorum Systems

So far, we have discussed quorum systems applicable in the context of crash failures. However, if node failures can be Byzantine [Lamport et al., 1982a], simple non-empty quorum intersections are not sufficient to guarantee consistency. Intuitively, if an intersection between two quorums contains, for example, a single process, and this process can be Byzantine, the Byzantine process can simply violate consistency. As an illustration (see Figure 5.1), assuming the Byzantine process is the sole process in the intersection of a write and a read quorum, it can simply "forget" seeing the write and cause inconsistencies in a read. To cope with this *Byzantine quorum systems* are employed in place of classical ones. Byzantine quorum systems have been widely used in asynchronous storage and consensus (replication) protocols, typically projected to the threshold failure model.

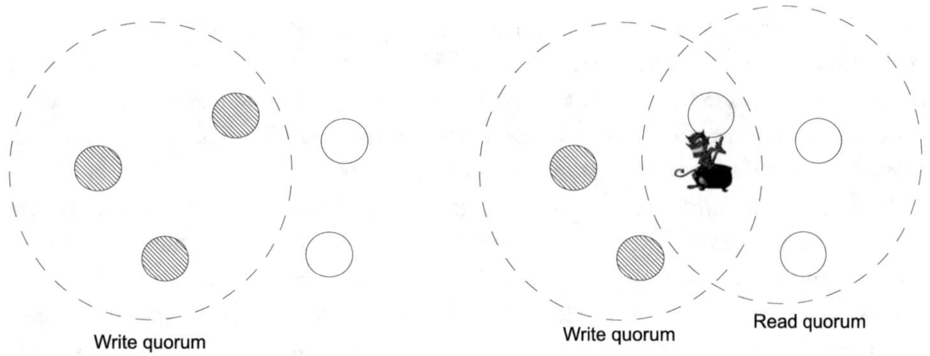

(a) A *write* to a quorum

(b) A subsequent *read* from a quorum containing a Byzantine process who "forgets" the *write*

Figure 5.1: Consistency violation with classical quorums in presence of Byzantine failures.

Byzantine quorum systems are specified not only with respect to a given set of processes S, but also assuming a specific set system over S called *monotone adversary*, or simply *adversary*.

Definition 5.1 Adversary Given a set S, a set system $\boldsymbol{B}$ is an adversary for S if and only if $B \in \boldsymbol{B} \wedge B' \subseteq B \Rightarrow B' \in \boldsymbol{B}$.

Remark 5.2 In the literature, a (monotone) adversary is also called *fail-prone set* [Malkhi and Reiter, 1998a] or *adversary structure* [Hirt and Maurer, 2000].

Intuitively, the adversary is defined to capture all possible combinations of simultaneously Byzantine processes. In the following, we assume that an adversary for S contains as its elements all possible subsets of S whose elements can be simultaneously Byzantine in any given execution.

Notation 5.3 Threshold adversary We denote by $\boldsymbol{B}_t$ a *threshold adversary* that contains all subsets of S of cardinality at most t, i.e.,

$$\boldsymbol{B}_t = \{Q \subseteq S : |Q| \leq t\}).$$

Armed with Definition 5.1, we are ready to define Byzantine quorum systems (BQS). We first describe three families of BQS, namely *dissemination* (Sec. 5.1), *masking* (Sec. 5.2) and *opaque* (Sec. 5.3) quorum systems [Malkhi and Reiter, 1998a]. Throughout the chapter, we describe several storage and consensus emulations that are based on these BQS.

5.1 DISSEMINATION QUORUM SYSTEMS

Dissemination quorum systems have initially been proposed [Malkhi and Reiter, 1998a] as quorum systems suitable for the authenticated Byzantine fault model. It is, however, possible to use dissemination quorum systems in the unauthenticated model as well, although, as we will see, the techniques used to make dissemination quorum systems work in the unauthenticated model are considerably more involved than their authenticated model counterparts.

We first define dissemination quorum systems and overview several basic results that apply to this class of quorum systems (Sec. 5.1.1). Then, we exemplify the use of dissemination quorum systems by two protocols: (1) a multi-writer multi-reader atomic storage emulation, called Phalanx, designed for the authenticated model [Malkhi and Reiter, 1998b]; and (2) a consensus emulation in the unauthenticated model, derived from the celebrated BFT replication protocol [Castro and Liskov, 2002].

5.1.1 BASICS

Definition 5.4 Dissemination quorum systems Given a set S and an adversary $\boldsymbol{B}$ for S, a quorum system (over S) $\boldsymbol{DQS}$ is a dissemination quorum system over S if and only if

(Byzantine intersection) $\forall Q_1, Q_2 \in \boldsymbol{DQS}, \forall B \in \boldsymbol{B} : Q_1 \cap Q_2 \nsubseteq B$.

Remark 5.5 In [Malkhi and Reiter, 1998a], dissemination quorum system are defined with an additional availability property requiring resilience to $\boldsymbol{B}$ (see Sec. 3.3.2). While this is clearly a necessary condition for the availability of a disseminating quorum system and the liveness of an underlying service, it may prohibit some applications which require a service to be safe, but not always live [Rodrigues et al., 2007]. Therefore, and to maintain generality, in this monograph we choose to separate the definitions of quorum systems (i.e., their intersection properties) from the availability considerations.

Dissemination quorum systems are necessary for any asynchronous storage or (eventually synchronous) consensus implementation. This is formally captured by the following Theorem.

Theorem 5.6 Let $\boldsymbol{BQS}$ be a coterie over set S and let $\boldsymbol{B}$ be an adversary S. Then, if there exists any asynchronous implementation of the single writer single reader (SWSR) safe storage based on $\boldsymbol{BQS}$, then $\boldsymbol{BQS}$ is a dissemination quorum system.

Remark 5.7 In the scope of Theorem 5.6, we focus on generic implementations that allow any process to be designated as the writer/reader. Hence, we rule out a certain class of implementations (e.g., in which a pre-selected process p is both reader and writer) which may lead to less interesting yet formally speaking correct implementations.

Proof. We prove the Theorem by assuming contradiction, i.e., that there is an SWSR safe storage emulation based on $\boldsymbol{BQS}$, such that $\boldsymbol{BQS}$ is not a dissemination quorum system.

Negating Definition 5.4 yields

$$\exists Q_1, Q_2 \in \boldsymbol{BQS}, \exists B \in \boldsymbol{B} : Q_1 \cap Q_2 \subseteq B \,. \qquad (1).$$

If (1) holds since $Q_1 = Q_2$, i.e., since $\exists Q_1 \in \boldsymbol{BQS} : Q_1 \subseteq B$, the proof is trivial. Therefore, we focus on the case where (1) holds for two distinct quorums in $\boldsymbol{BQS}$, $Q_1 \neq Q_2$. The proof is illustrated in Figure 5.2.

Assume by contradiction that a SWSR storage implementation I exists. Since $\boldsymbol{BQS}$ is a coterie, $Q_1 \setminus Q_2 \neq \emptyset$ and $Q_2 \setminus Q_1 \neq \emptyset$. Denote by p_1 a process in $Q_1 \setminus Q_2$ and by p_2 a process in $Q_2 \setminus Q_1$. Let p_1 be the writer and p_2 be the reader. Let $B_2' = B \setminus \{p_2\}$. Notice that since $Q_1 \cap Q_2 \subseteq B$ and $p_2 \notin Q_1$, we have $Q_1 \cap Q_2 \subseteq B_2'$. Fix $B_2 \subseteq B_2'$ such that $Q_1 \cap Q_2 = B_2$. By Definition 5.1, since $B_2 \subseteq B_2' \subseteq B$, we have $B_2 \in \boldsymbol{B}$.

Let ex_1 be the partial execution in which all processes in the system crash at the beginning of the execution except processes from Q_1. Moreover, in ex_1, p_1 invokes $write(v)$. By Definition 4.1 and since there is a quorum that contains only correct processes (Q_1) and $write(v)$ eventually completes in ex_1.

Let ex_2 be a different partial execution in which all processes in the system crash at the beginning of the execution, except processes from Q_2. Moreover, in ex_2, p_2 invokes $read()$. Due to our assumption on I and since there is a quorum that contains only correct processes (Q_2), $read$ by p_2 eventually completes in ex_2. By definition of the safe register $read$ by p_2 returns $\perp$.

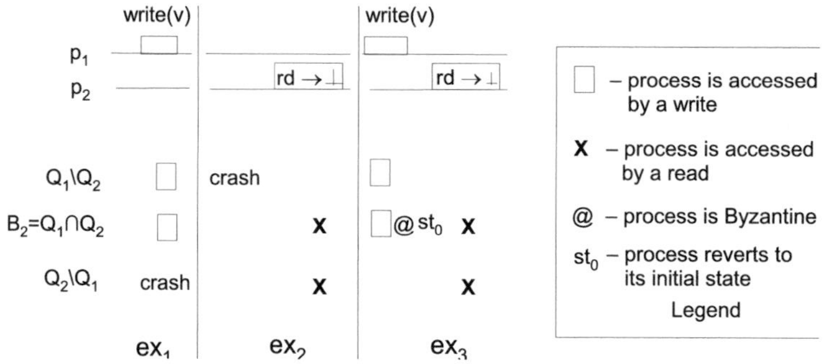

Figure 5.2: Executions illustrating the proof of Theorem 5.6. Only processes that belong to $Q_1 \cup Q_2$ are depicted.

Now consider partial execution ex_3, in which processes from B_2 are *Byzantine*, the remaining processes from $Q_1 \cup Q_2$ are correct and all other processes crash at the beginning of the execution. Moreover, in ex_3, due to asynchrony, messages sent by processes from $Q_1 \setminus Q_2$ are not delivered to processes from $Q_2 \setminus Q_1$ (this is possible, since ex_3 is a finite, partial run).

In ex_3, p_1 invokes $write(v)$, just like in ex_1. Byzantine processes from B_2 follow the protocol of I during $write(v)$. Hence, correct processes from Q_1 cannot distinguish ex_3 from ex_1 and $write(v)$ eventually completes in ex_3 at time t. At time $t' > t$ processes from B_2 exhibit a Byzantine fault by reverting their state to the initial one.[1] After t', processes from B_2 follow the protocol, except that they do not receive any message from correct processes from Q_1. Finally, at time $t'' > t'$, p_2 invokes a *read* operation. Process p_2 cannot distinguish ex_3 from ex_2 and eventually *read* completes and returns $\perp$. A violation of safeness. □

It is not difficult to extend the Theorem 5.6 to show that a similar result applies for eventually synchronous consensus implementations. We leave this as an exercise.

A special and particularly important case of dissemination quorum systems are t-dissemination quorum system.

Definition 5.8 **$t-$dissemination quorum systems** Given the adversary $\boldsymbol{B}_t$, a dissemination quorum system is a t-dissemination quorum system if its resilience is at least t.

The following Lemma can derived directly from the definition of a threshold adversary $\boldsymbol{B}_t$.

Lemma 5.9 *In a t-dissemination quorum system $\boldsymbol{tDQS}$, all quorums intersect in at least $t+1$ elements.*

[1] Notice that this action by a Byzantine process is possible in both authenticated and unauthenticated Byzantine fault models

The following Lemma stipulates the lower bound on the number of processes in a set over which a $t-$dissemination quorum system can be constructed.

Lemma 5.10 *No t-dissemination quorum system can be constructed over S if $n = |S| \leq 3t$.*

Proof. Assume by contradiction that there is a $t-$dissemination quorum system $\boldsymbol{tDQS}$ over a set of processes of cardinality $n \leq 3t$. Then, by Definition 3.22, it is not difficult to see that $\boldsymbol{tDQS}$ cannot contain a single quorum. Hence, there are two quorums $Q_1, Q_2 \in \boldsymbol{tDQS}$ such that $|Q_1| \leq n-t$, $|Q_2| \leq n-t$ and $|Q_2 \setminus Q_1| = t$. Therefore, $|Q_1 \cap Q_2| \leq n - 2t \leq t$, i.e., $Q_1 \cap Q_2 \in \boldsymbol{B_t}$. A contradiction (Def. 5.4, Def. 5.8). □

The following theorem gives the lower bound on the load of any t-dissemination quorum system [Malkhi et al., 2000].

Theorem 5.11 Lower bound on load $\mathcal{L}(\boldsymbol{tDQS}) \geq \sqrt{\frac{t+1}{n}}$ for any t-dissemination quorum system $\boldsymbol{tDQS}$.

Proof. Let σ be any strategy and fix $Q_i \in \boldsymbol{tDQS}$ such that $|Q_i| = m(\boldsymbol{tDQS})$.

$$\sum_{s_i \in Q_i} l_\sigma(s_i, \boldsymbol{tDQS}) \stackrel{\text{Def. 3.11}}{=} \sum_{s_i \in Q_i} \sum_{Q \ni s_i} \sigma_{\boldsymbol{tDQS}}(Q) = \sum_{Q} \sum_{s_i \in Q \cap Q_i} \sigma_{\boldsymbol{tDQS}}(Q)$$

$$\stackrel{\text{Lemma 5.9}}{\geq} \sum_{Q} (t+1)\sigma_{\boldsymbol{tDQS}}(Q) \stackrel{\text{Def. 3.3}}{=} t+1$$

which implies that at least one element of Q_i suffers the load of at least $\frac{t+1}{m(\boldsymbol{tDQS})}$. In case $m(\boldsymbol{tDQS}) \leq \sqrt{(t+1)n}$, the Theorem follows. On the other hand, in case $m(\boldsymbol{tDQS}) \geq \sqrt{(t+1)n}$, the theorem follows from:

$$\sum_{s_i \in S} l_\sigma(s_i, \boldsymbol{tDQS}) \stackrel{\text{Def. 3.11}}{=} \sum_{s_i \in S} \sum_{Q \ni s_i} \sigma_{\boldsymbol{tDQS}}(Q) = \sum_{Q} |Q| \sigma_{\boldsymbol{tDQS}}(Q)$$

$$\geq \sum_{Q} m(\boldsymbol{tDQS}) \sigma_{\boldsymbol{tDQS}}(Q) \stackrel{\text{Def. 3.3}}{=} m(\boldsymbol{tDQS})$$

which implies that at least one element of S suffers the load of at least $\frac{m(\boldsymbol{tDQS})}{n}$. □

Examples. If $n = 3t + 1$, an example of a t-dissemination quorum system is a two-thirds majority quorum system:

$$\boldsymbol{Maj}_{\frac{2}{3}} = \{Q \subseteq S : |Q| = n - t = 2t + 1\}.$$

$\boldsymbol{Maj}_{\frac{2}{3}}$ is optimally resilient quorum system, with the resilience expressed as a function of n:

$$\mathcal{R}(\boldsymbol{Maj}_{\frac{2}{3}}) = \left\lfloor \frac{n-1}{3} \right\rfloor.$$

More generally, for $n > 3t$,

$$\boldsymbol{DQS}_t = \left\{ Q \subseteq S : |Q| = \left\lceil \frac{n+t+1}{2} \right\rceil \right\}$$

is a t-dissemination quorum system.

The load of $\mathbf{DQS_t}$ is

$$\mathcal{L}(\mathbf{DQS_t}) = \frac{1}{n} \left\lceil \frac{n+t+1}{2} \right\rceil.$$

5.1.2 STORAGE EMULATION

Dissemination quorum systems, with the addition of digital signatures, can be used in place of classical quorum systems in the generalized ABD algorithm (Sec. 4.1) to obtain Phalanx [Malkhi and Reiter, 1998a], a multi-writer multi-reader atomic storage emulation that assumes the authenticated Byzantine fault model. Hence, Phalanx complements Theorem 5.6 proving that the Byzantine intersection property of dissemination quorum systems is not only necessary but also sufficient for implementing Byzantine fault-tolerant storage.

In Phalanx, we assume that every writer can produce digital signatures, whereas all processes can verify these signatures. In a sense, Phalanx is a hardened variant of ABD. Namely, Phalanx is exactly the same as ABD except that:

1. Phalanx makes use of digital signatures for message authentication as well as associated verification procedure.

2. Phalanx is based on dissemination quorum systems instead on classical ones. More specifically, Phalanx assumes a dissemination quorum system $\boldsymbol{DQS}$ over a set of servers and is wait-free if a quorum in $\boldsymbol{DQS}$ contains only correct processes.

3. Finally, Phalanx assumes writers not to be Byzantine, although writers may fail by crashing. On the other hand, clients who invoke solely *read* operations (i.e., the readers) may be Byzantine.

The client and server protocols are given in Algorithms 14 and 15, respectively.

In our description of Phalanx, we focus on differences with respect to ABD (Sec. 4.1). Phalanx differs from ABD in utilization of digital signatures by clients who invoke *write* operation. In line 9

Algorithm 14 Phalanx algorithm (client c pseudocode)

Local variables initialization: $opCnt \leftarrow 0; maxts \leftarrow 0; maxc \leftarrow 0; maxval \leftarrow \perp; maxsig \leftarrow \perp$

```
upon inv_c(Phalanx, write(v)) do
  opCnt ← opCnt + 1
  Phase 1:                                                   {Timestamp synchronization}
    send (read, opCnt) to all servers
    when receive (readack, val_i, ⟨ts_i, cid_i⟩, sig_i, opCnt) and V(c_i, (val_i, ts_i, cid_i), sig_i)
    from all s_i from some Q ∈ DQS
      maxts ← maximum ts_i in received readack messages
    end when
  Phase 2:                                                   {Write}
    send (write, v, ⟨maxts + 1, c⟩, σ_c(v, maxts + 1, c), opCnt) to all servers
    when receive (writeack, opCnt) from all s_i from some Q ∈ DQS
      return resp_c(Phalanx, ack)
    end when
end upon
```

```
upon inv_c(Phalanx, read()) do
  opCnt ← opCnt + 1
  Phase 1:                                                   {Read}
    send (read, opCnt) to all servers
    when receive (readack, val_i, ⟨ts_i, cid_i⟩, sig_i, opCnt) and V(c_i, (val_i, ts_i, cid_i), sig_i)
    from all s_i from some Q ∈ DQS
      maxts ← maximum ts_i in received readack messages
      maxcid ← maximum cid_i in received readack messages with maxts
      maxval ← val_i in received readack message with ⟨maxts, maxcid⟩
      maxsig ← sig_i in received readack message with ⟨maxts, maxcid⟩
    end when
  Phase 2:                                                   {Writeback}
    send (write, maxval, ⟨maxts, maxcid⟩, maxsig, opCnt) to all servers
    when receive (writeack, opCnt) from all s_i from some Q ∈ DQS
      return resp_c(Phalanx, maxval)
    end when
end upon
```

Algorithm 15 Phalanx algorithm (server s_i pseudocode)

Local variables initialization: $tag_i[ts, cid] = \langle 0, 0\rangle$; $val_i \leftarrow \bot$; $sig_i \leftarrow \bot$;

1: **upon** $receive\ (read, cnt)$ from client c **do**
2: $\quad send(readack, val_i, tag_i, sig_i, cnt)$ to c
3: **end upon**
4: **upon** $receive\ (write, val', \langle ts', cid'\rangle, sig', cnt)$ from client c **and** $V(c', (val', ts', c'), sig')$ **do**
5: $\quad$ **if** $ts' > tag_i.ts$ **or** $(ts' = tag_i.ts$ **and** $cid' > tag_i.cid)$ **then**
6: $\quad\quad tag_i \leftarrow \langle ts', cid'\rangle$; $val_i \leftarrow val'$; $sig_i \leftarrow sig'$
7: $\quad$ **end if**
8: $\quad send(writeack, cnt)$ to c
9: **end upon**

of Algorithm 14, a writer adds to the ABD $write$ its digital signature sig on the triple $(v, maxts + 1, c)$, i.e., $sig = \sigma_c(v, maxts + 1, c)$, where c denotes the writer's id. Upon a server s_i receives a $write$ message from writer c, s_i verifies the signature sig before acting on the message (line 4, Algorithm 15), by invoking $V(c, (v, maxts + 1, c), sig)$. If the signature verification succeeds (and the value in the $write$ message is newer than server's locally stored copy), a correct server updates its local copy of the value and timestamp, and stores the signature as well (line 6, Algorithm 15).

A correct server uses the locally stored signature along with the local value and timestamp in $readack$ in response to a $read$ message (line 2, Algorithm 15). The signature is again verified by clients upon reception of a $readack$ message (lines 5 and 18, Algorithm 14).[2] This technique serves to discard values possibly forged by a Byzantine server.

Finally, when a reader writesback the value (line 25, Algorithm 14) it includes the signature that it received in the $readack$ message with the highest timestamp (line 22, Algorithm 14). Notice that the signature included by a reader in the $write$ message of the writeback phase is a signature of a *writer* that wrote the value the reader selected to return. Hence, readers do not produce signatures but rather help propagate writers' signature to a quorum of server. This technique guarantees that Phalanx can tolerate Byzantine readers.

It is not difficult to adapt the correctness proof of ABD (Lemma 4.2) to prove Phalanx atomic, by relying on the unforgeability of digital signatures and by replacing the reasoning about the classic quorum Intersection property with the Byzantine intersection property of Definition 5.4.

[2] To cover initial storage state, we assume that $V(0, (\bot, 0, 0), \bot)$ evaluates to $true$.

5.1.3 CONSENSUS EMULATION

In this section we present CL, a consensus protocol in the authenticated Byzantine fault model derived from the PBFT state-machine replication protocol [Castro and Liskov, 2002]. Like Phalanx, CL relies on dissemination quorum systems and digital signatures to cope with Byzantine faults. More specifically, we assume a dissemination quorum system $\boldsymbol{DQS}$ and adversary $\boldsymbol{B}$ over a set of $acceptors$ such that, in every execution a quorum of acceptors is available (i.e., $\exists Q \in \boldsymbol{DQS} : Q \subseteq alive(acceptors)$). Besides, CL tolerates any number of Byzantine proposers. CL can be seen as the Byzantine variant of the Synod consensus protocol (Sec. 4.2) in the eventually synchronous model.

5.1.3.1 Overview

The CL algorithm consists of two modules: (1) a *Locking* module that ensures consensus safety properties (i.e., Validity and Agreement); and (2) an *Election* module used to help ensure liveness (i.e., Termination). Roughly speaking, the Locking module in CL corresponds to SynodOFC in Synod, whereas the Election module is an implementation of the eventual leader failure detector Ω.

Furthermore, like SynodOFC, the Locking module consists of a *NewView* and an *Update* phase, corresponding to Phases 1 and 2 of SynodOFC, respectively.

The wrap-up, high-level code of a proposer is given in Algorithm 16. We assume that every proposer p is initialized with an initial proposal value v_p

Algorithm 16 CL implementation using Locking and Election modules (proposer p pseudocode)

Local variables initialization: $view \leftarrow 0; initView \leftarrow 0; propView \leftarrow -1$

upon $inv_p(CL, propose(v))$ **do**
    loop
        upon ($view = initView$ **or** p is output by the Election module) **and** $propView < view$ **do**
            $propView \leftarrow view$
            $inv_p(Locking, propose(v))$
        end upon
    end loop
end upon

CL algorithm proceeds in a sequence of *views*. View numbers take values from $\mathbb{N}_0$ and, roughly speaking, can be seen as a variant of Synod ballot numbers. In every view w, except in the initial view 0 (denoted by $initView$) a single proposer is the *leader*. Leaders are elected by the *Election* module following a round robin fashion (i.e., the leader of view $w \neq initView$ is proposer p_i, where $i = w \bmod \mathcal{P}$).

A value is proposed in CL within the Locking module (line 5, Algorithm 16 and Algorithm 17). On proposing a value in a view $w \neq initView$, the leader invokes the NewView phase which (just like Phase 1 in SynodOFC) ensures that p_i changes its proposal value to v_l in case v_l was already *chosen*, i.e., if some benign learner learned v_l in some of the previous views. After the NewView phase, the leader invokes the Update phase of the Locking module.

The special case is the initial view, $initView$, in which all proposers can be seen as leaders and are allowed to propose values. As shown in Algorithm 17 (line 3), in $initView$, a proposer skips the NewView phase and proceeds directly to the Update phase. Hence, in the following we focus first on explaining the Update phase of the Locking module. Then, we turn to the NewView phase with the particular focus on how CL ensures that the chosen value is the only value that can be successfully proposed by a leader in the NewView phase. Finally, we give a simple implementation of the *Election* module.

5.1.3.2 Update phase

Update phase of the Locking module proceeds in three communication steps, in contrast to two communication steps in Phase 2 of SynodOFC. We follow these communication steps (depicted in Figure 5.3) meanwhile explaining all the variables that processes maintain:

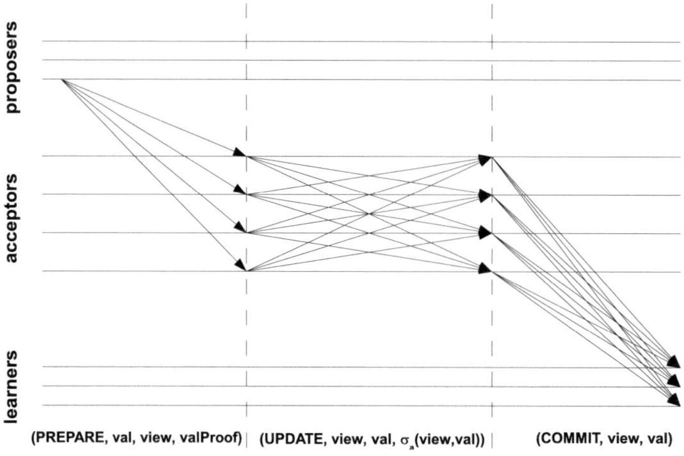

Figure 5.3: CL algorithm: message pattern of the Update phase of the Locking module.

1. Proposer p sends a $\langle prepare, val, view, valProof \rangle$ message (line 20, Algorithm 17) containing:

Algorithm 17 Locking module implementation (pseudocode of proposer p)

Local variables initialization: $viewProof \leftarrow nil$; $proof \leftarrow nil$; $valProof \leftarrow nil$;
  $faultyQuorums \leftarrow \emptyset$; $val \leftarrow \bot$; $correct \leftarrow false$

1: **upon** $inv_p(Locking, propose(v))$ **do**
2:    $val \leftarrow v$
3:    **if** $view > initView$ **then**
4:      **Phase 1:**   *{NewView phase}*
5:        $send(newView, view, viewProof)$ to all acceptors
6:        **while** $\neg correct$ **do**
7:          **when** $receive\ (newViewAck, view, v_i, updateView_i, updateProof_i)$ from all a_i from some $Q \in DQS \setminus faultyQuorums$
8:            $proof \leftarrow$ the set of received $newViewAck$ messages from Q
9:            **if isValid**(m_i, a_i) for all $m_i \in proof$ and matching $a_i \in Q$ **then**
10:              $val \leftarrow$ **leaderSelect**$(proof, val, v)$
11:              $valProof \leftarrow proof$
12:              $correct \leftarrow true$
13:            **else**
14:              $faultyQuorums \leftarrow faultyQuorums \cup \{Q\}$
15:            **end if**
16:          **end when**
17:        **end while**
18:      **end if**
19:      **Phase 2:**   *{Update phase}*
20:        $send(prepare, val, view, valProof)$ to all acceptors
21: **end upon**
22: **function leaderSelect**$(msgs, val, v)$
23:    $maxview \leftarrow$ maximum $m.updateView_i$ for all $m \in msgs$
24:    $maxval \leftarrow m.v_i$ for $m \in msgs$ with $m.updateView_i = maxview$
25:    **if** $maxval \neq \bot$ **then**
26:      **return** $maxval$
27:    **else**
28:      **return** v
29:    **end if**
30: **end function**

Algorithm 18 Locking module implementation (acceptor a pseudocode)

Local variables initialization: $initView \leftarrow 0$; $localView \leftarrow 0$; $prepareView \leftarrow -1$; $preparedValue \leftarrow \bot$; $updateView \leftarrow -1$; $updateProof \leftarrow \emptyset$; $v \leftarrow \bot$; $pendingProof \leftarrow \emptyset$; $updatedAcceptors \leftarrow \emptyset$

1: **upon** $receive\ m = (newView, view, viewProof)$ from some proposer p **do**
2:   **if** **isValid**(m, p) **and** $view > localView$ **then**
3:     $localView \leftarrow view$
4:     $pendingProof \leftarrow \emptyset$
5:     $updatedAcceptors \leftarrow \emptyset$
6:     $send(newViewAck, localView, v, updateView, updateProof)$ to p
7:   **end if**
8: **end upon**

9: **upon** $receive\ m = (prepare, val, localView, valProof)$ from some proposer p **do**
10:   **if** $(localView = initView$ **or** $(val = \textbf{leaderSelect}(valProof, val, val)$ **and** $p = view$ mod $\mathcal{P})$ **and** $prepView < localView$ **then**
11:     $prepV \leftarrow val$; $prepView \leftarrow localView$
12:     $send(update, localView, prepV, \sigma_a(localView, prepV))$ to all acceptors
13:   **end if**
14: **end upon**

15: **upon** $receive$ $m = (update, prepareView, prepV, sig)$ from   some   acceptor a' **and** $prepareView = localView$ **do**
16:   **if** $updateView < prepareView$ **and** $V(a', (prepareView, val), sig)$ **then**
17:     $updatedAcceptors \leftarrow updatedAcceptors \cup \{a'\}$
18:     $pendingProof \leftarrow pendingProof \cup \{m\}$
19:     **if** $updatedAcceptors = Q$ for some $Q \in DQS$ **then**
20:       $updateView \leftarrow prepareView$
21:       $updateProof \leftarrow pendingProof$
22:       $v \leftarrow prepV$
23:       $send(commit, updateView, v)$ to all learners
24:     **end if**
25:   **end if**
26: **end upon**

Algorithm 19 Locking module implementation (learner l pseudocode)

```
upon receive (commit, view, v) from all a_i from some Q ∈ DQS do
    return learn(v)
end upon
```

(a) proposal value val;

(b) the view number $view$; and

(c) the array of authenticated messages $valProof$ that originates from some quorum Q of acceptors.

Roughly, $valProof$ serves as a certificate for the proposed value val and limits the ability of a Byzantine proposer to propose any value. We detail how $valProof$ is constructed later when explaining the *NewView* phase. Notice that, in $initView$, $valProof$ contains no messages (i.e., $valProof = nil$).

2. Benign acceptor a, upon receiving $(prepare, val, view, valProof)$ from p (line 9, Algorithm 18), such that $view$ equals $localView$ variable which uniquely determines the view number in which acceptor a participates, checks (line 10, Algorithm 18):

   (a) whether p is the leader of $view$; this check is omitted in case $view = initView$,

   (b) whether $vProof$ matches value val; this is done using the $leaderSelect()$ function that is explained later in details, and

   (c) whether acceptor a had not prepared a value in $localView$, i.e., if a makes sure its local variable $prepView$ is smaller than $localView$.

   If these checks succeed, a *prepares* the value val in $localView$, i.e., a stores val into local variable $prepV$, as well as $localView$ in $prepView$. Then, a echoes v by sending a $(update, localView, prepV, \sigma_a(localView, prepV))$ to all acceptors (line 12, Algorithm 18). Notice that when a sends $update$ messages, these contain a's digital signature on the pair $(localView, prepV)$.

3. Benign acceptor a, upon receiving $m = (update, view, val, sig)$ from some acceptor a', such that $view = prepView$ and $val = prepV$ and if a already prepared a value in $localView$, i.e., if $localView = prepView$, (line 15, Algorithm 18), makes sure that (line 16, Algorithm 18):

   (a) a had not already updated a value in $localView$, i.e., if a's local variable $updateView$ is smaller than $prepView = localView$;

   (b) (b) a verifies the signature in the $update$ message (i.e., checks if $V(a', (prepareView, val), sig)$ holds).

If these checks succeed, a adds a' to its (initially empty) local set $updatedAcceptors$ and message m into (also initially empty) local set $pendingProof$. Once $updatedAcceptors$ contains a quorum $Q \in \boldsymbol{DQS}$ of acceptors (line 19, Algorithm 18), a *updates* $prepV$ in $localView$, i.e., stores $prepV$ into its main local variable v, $pendingProof$ into $updateProof$, and $localView = prepareView$ into $updateView$. Finally, upon updating v in $localView$, a sends a sends a $(commit, updateView, v)$ message to all learners (line 12, Algorithm 18).

4. Finally, a benign learner l, upon receiving $(commit, view, v)$ message with identical $view$ and v from some quorum of acceptors $Q \in \boldsymbol{DQS}$, learns v (Algorithm 18).

5.1.3.3 *NewView* phase

Election module, responsible for view changes and leader election might designate some proposer p to be the leader of some $view > initView$. As we will see later, such a proposer p receives the voucher from Election module in the form of $viewProof$ which guarantees that a Byzantine proposer cannot pretend that it is the leader of $view$. If p is benign and elected, it will invoke the new proposal to the Locking module and execute first the *NewView* phase of the *Locking* module (since $view > initView$). NewView phase includes two communication steps involving p and acceptors:

1. Proposer p starts the *NewView* phase of a new view $view$ by sending the $(newView, view, viewProof)$ message to acceptors (line 5, Algorithm 17).

2. Upon receiving $m = (newView, view, viewProof)$ message from p, An acceptor a checks if (line 2, Algorithm 18):

   (a) $view$ is higher than a's local view number $localView$; and

   (b) if m is *valid*, i.e., if p is indeed the leader of $view$, i.e., if $viewProof$ provided by the Election module contains a quorum of authenticated messages vouching that p may issue a $newView$ message for $view$.

   If these checks succeed, a joins $view$ by storing it in $localView$ and empties its local $pendingProof$ and $updatedAcceptors$ sets. After joining $view$, a replies with $(newViewAck, localView, v, updateView, updateProof)$ to p (line 6, Algorithm 17), hence informing the proposer of its last updated value v and corresponding view number $updateView$, along with the $updateProof$, i.e., the proof that vouches that a could have updated v.

3. After sending the $(newView, view, viewProof)$ message, p_i waits for a quorum Q of *valid* $(newViewAck, view, v, updateView, updateProof)$ messages (line 9, Algorithm 17). Such a message received from an acceptor a is considered valid, if $updateProof$ vouches for v and $updateView$, i.e., if a indeed updated v in $updateView$. Since, $updateProof$ consists of a set of $(update, view', val', sig')$ messages from some quorum Q of acceptors, this involves checking, for every message $m \in updateProof$, if $view' = updateView$,

$val' = v$ and if every sig' is indeed a digital signature on the pair $(view', val')$. As we will see this prohibits Byzantine acceptors to forge v with high $updateView$, that would compromise the correctness of CL.

Upon successful check, p as the leader of $view$, selects a proposal value val using the **leaderSelect** function (line 10, Algorithm 17) which is a faithful port of the **leaderSelect** procedure in SynodOFC (see also Algorithm 6): namely, p simply picks the value v with the highest $updateView$, among the received valid $newViewAck$ messages. If such a value turns out to be $\perp$, the leader sticks with its initial proposal value (lines 22-30, Algorithm 17). Finally, p stores the received $newViewAck$ messages from quorum Q in its $valProof$ variable, in order to prove to acceptors in the subsequent Update phase, that it is not Byzantine and that it has properly selected the proposal value in $view$.

5.1.3.4 The *Election* module

For completeness, the Election module given in Algorithm 20. This module is based on exponential increase of timeouts and gives a very simple eventual leader failure detector implementation in the eventually synchronous authenticated Byzantine fault model. Different optimizations of this simple scheme are possible, but these are out of the scope of this monograph.

As we already mentioned, Election module supplies proposer p executing the Locking module with $viewProof$, the proof that p is a legitimate leader of $view$. As evident from simple inspection of Algorithm 20, $viewProof$ contains a quorum of digital signatures on view number from different acceptors.

5.1.3.5 Correctness arguments

Once again we focus on arguments evolving around the Agreement property of consensus. These arguments critically depend on the Byzantine intersection property of dissemination quorum systems that underlie CL.

Definition 5.12 Learning in view If some learner learns value v by receiving a quorum of $(commit, view, v)$ messages, we say that a learner learns v in $view$.

Definition 5.13 Choosing in view If a quorum of acceptors updates v in $view$, we say that v is *chosen* in $view$.

The proof of the following Lemma is straightforward.

Lemma 5.14 *If a learner learns v in $view$, then v is chosen in $view$.*

The following two Lemmas with the proofs based on dissemination quorum intersections, are crucial in arguing about consensus Agreement in CL.

Lemma 5.15 *No two benign acceptors can update different values in the same view.*

Algorithm 20 Election module implementation

code of acceptor a

Local variables initialization:

$suspectTimeout, initTimeout \leftarrow 5\Delta; nextView \leftarrow initView; nextLeader \leftarrow 0$

1: **upon** *receive* a *prepare* message for the first time **do**
2:    **trigger**($suspectTimeout$)
3: **end upon**
4: **upon** expiration of $suspectTimeout$ **do**
5:    $suspectTimeout \leftarrow suspectTimeout * 2$
6:    $nextView \leftarrow nextView + 1$
7:    $nextLeader \leftarrow nextView \bmod \mathcal{P}$
8:    *send* $(viewChange, nextView, \sigma_a nextView)$ to proposer $p_{nextLeader}$
9:    **trigger**($suspectTimeout$)
10: **end upon**
11: **upon** *receive* $m = (newView, view, viewProof)$ from proposer p **and isValid**(m, p) **do**
12:    $nextView \leftarrow view$
13:    $suspectTimeout \leftarrow initTimeout * 2^{view}$
14: **end upon**

---

code of proposer p

1: **upon** *receive* $(viewChange, nextView, sig_i)$ **and** $V(a_i, (nextView), sig_i)$ from all acceptors a_i from some $Q \in \boldsymbol{DQS}$ **do**
2:    **if** $nextView > view$ **then**
3:       $viewProof \leftarrow$ the set of received $viewChange$ messages from Q
4:       $view \leftarrow nextView$
5:       **elect**(p)
6:    **end if**
7: **end upon**

Proof. *(Sketch)* Notice first that no benign acceptor a prepares nor updates more than one value in a given view. Moreover, if a benign acceptor a updates v in $view$, then a prepares v in $view$. Then, the lemma immediately follows from the fact that benign acceptor a only if it receives a quorum of $update$ messages, meaning that a updates v in $view$, only if a quorum of acceptors prepared v in $view$. Hence, by the Byzantine intersection property of Definition 5.4, the Lemma follows. □

Corollary 5.16 *No two different values can be chosen in the same* $view$.

Lemma 5.17 *If a value* v *is chosen in* $view$*, then a benign acceptor can only prepare* v *in views higher than* $view$.

Proof. *(Sketch)* The proof of this lemma proceeds by induction on view numbers higher than $view$. Here we give arguments for the base step, i.e., we argue that if a value v is chosen in $view$, then a benign acceptor can only prepare v in $view + 1$. The induction step is very similar to the base step and is left as an exercise.

By Definition 5.13, if v was chosen in $view$, then a quorum $Q \in \boldsymbol{DQS}$ of acceptors updated v in $view$. When the leader of $view + 1$ executes the NewView phase of the Locking module, it contacts a quorum $Q' \in \boldsymbol{DQS}$ of acceptors. By Byzantine intersection property of Definition 5.4, $Q \cap Q'$ contains at least one benign acceptor a.

Notice that a updates v in $view$ before it replies to the leader of $view + 1$ in the NewView phase of $view + 1$. Hence, the $(newViewAck, view + 1, v, updateView, updateProof)$ message send by a to the leader of $view + 1$ is such that $updateView = view$. By our assumption on digital signatures, no Byzantine acceptor in Q' can send a valid $newViewAck$ message with higher $updateView$ number than $view$. Hence, in the **leaderSelect** function parameterized by the set of $newViewAck$ messages received by the leader of $view + 1$ from Q', the highest $updateView$ number will in fact be $view$. By Lemma 5.15 and our assumption on the unforgeability of digital signatures, there cannot be two different $newViewAck$ messages with different values yet with the same $updateView = view$. Hence, **leaderSelect** must return v. □

5.2 MASKING QUORUM SYSTEMS

Besides dissemination quorum systems, [Malkhi and Reiter, 1998a] also proposed *masking* quorum systems with the goal of storing *unauthenticated* data. As we already discussed earlier, relying on masking quorum systems to store unauthenticated data revealed not to be necessary, because unauthenticated data can be stored in a consistent manner using dissemination quorum systems only. However, designing storage protocols for storing unauthenticated data is arguably much simpler when using masking instead of dissemination quorum systems.

In the following, we first define, in Sec. 5.2.1, masking quorum systems and overview basic theorems that give the intuition behind the complexity of using non-masking quorum systems in the unauthenticated model. Then, in Sec. 5.2.2 we give a simple example of using masking quorum systems for storage emulation in an unauthenticated model. More specifically, we give the classical single-writer multi-reader safe storage emulation, called MR [Malkhi and Reiter, 1998a].

5.2.1 BASICS

Masking quorum systems are defined as follows.

Definition 5.18 Masking quorum systems Given a set S and an adversary $\boldsymbol{B}$ for S, a quorum system (over S) $\boldsymbol{MQS}$ is a masking quorum system over S if and only if

(M-Byzantine intersection) $\forall Q_1, Q_2 \in \boldsymbol{MQS}, \forall B_1, B_2 \in \boldsymbol{B} : Q_1 \cap Q_2 \not\subseteq B_1 \cup B_2$.

Given the above definition, it is straightforward to see that masking quorums are a further refinement of dissemination quorums: all masking quorum systems are also dissemination quorum systems, but, the opposite does not hold.

Analogously to t-dissemination quorum systems, we can define t-masking quorum systems. These are masking quorum system that are most often used in practice.

Definition 5.19 t−masking quorum systems Given the adversary $\boldsymbol{B}_t$, a masking quorum system is a t-masking quorum system if its resilience is at least t.

Example. For $n > 4t$, it can be shown [Malkhi and Reiter, 1998a] that $\mathbf{MQS_t} = \left\{Q \subseteq S : |Q| = \left\lceil \frac{n+2t+1}{2} \right\rceil\right\}$ is a t-masking quorum system. The load of this quorum system is $\mathcal{L}(\mathbf{MQS_t}) = \frac{1}{n}\left\lceil \frac{n+2t+1}{2} \right\rceil$ and is achieved by the strategy that assigns uniform probabilities across all quorums.

The following results applicable to masking quorum systems can be easily shown using the proofs of the similar results proved in Sec. 5.1.1 in the context of dissemination quorum systems.

Lemma 5.20 *In a t-masking quorum system $\boldsymbol{tMQS}$, all quorums intersect in at least $2t+1$ elements.*

Lemma 5.21 *No t-masking quorum system can be constructed over S if $n = |S| \leq 4t$.*

Theorem 5.22 Load $\mathcal{L}(\boldsymbol{tMQS}) \geq \sqrt{\frac{2t+1}{n}}$ for any t-masking quorum system $\boldsymbol{tMQS}$.

We now prove a fundamental result that shows that masking quorum systems are necessary for fast, *single-round* implementations of distributed storage in the unauthenticated model. Informally, the notion of a single-round implementation relates to an implementation in which *read*/*write* operations access quorums only once (to access an element of a quorum and to receive a reply), even in the worst case. Single-round implementations can also be defined with respect to their time complexity as follows:

Definition 5.23 Single-round storage A storage implementation is a *single-round* one if the worst-case latency of *write* or *read* is two message delays.

The necessity of masking quorum systems for single-round storage implementations in the unauthenticated Byzantine failure model is captured in the following theorem.

Theorem 5.24 Let $\boldsymbol{BQS}$ be a coterie over set S and let $\boldsymbol{B}$ be an adversary S. Then, if there exists any asynchronous implementation in the unauthenticated Byzantine failure model of the single writer single reader (SWSR) single-round safe storage based on $\boldsymbol{BQS}$, then $\boldsymbol{BQS}$ is a masking quorum system.

Proof. The proof proceeds assuming a contradiction, i.e., the existence of a SWSR single round storage implementation that is based on a coterie $\boldsymbol{BQS}$ which is not a masking quorum system.

Negating Definition 5.18 yields:

$$\exists Q_1, Q_2 \in \boldsymbol{BQS}, \exists B, B' \in \boldsymbol{B} : Q_1 \cap Q_2 \subseteq B \cup B' . \qquad (1).$$

By Definition 5.1, we can fix $B_1 \subseteq B$ and $B_2 \subseteq B'$, such that $B_1, B_2 \in \boldsymbol{B}$, $B_1 \cap B_2 = \emptyset$ and $Q_1 \cap Q_2 = B_1 \cup B_2$.

We focus on the case where (1) holds for two distinct quorums in $\boldsymbol{BQS}$, $Q_1 \neq Q_2$. In case (1) holds since $Q_1 = Q_2$, the proof is a rather straightforward variant of the $Q_1 \neq Q_2$ case.

Since $\boldsymbol{BQS}$ is a coterie, $Q_1 \setminus Q_2 \neq \emptyset$ and $Q_2 \setminus Q_1 \neq \emptyset$. Denote by p_1 be a process in $Q_1 \setminus Q_2$ and by p_2 a process in $Q_2 \setminus Q_1$. Let p_1 be the writer and p_2 be the reader. Notice that $p_1, p_2 \notin B_1 \cup B_2$.[3]

We illustrate the executions used in this proof in Figure 5.4. In the illustration set T_1 stands for the set $Q_1 \setminus (Q_2 \cup \{p_1\})$, whereas $T_2 = Q_2 \setminus (Q_1 \cup \{p_2\})$.

First, assume by contradiction that a SWSR storage implementation I in which the worst-case latency of *write* is two message delays exists (illustrations are given in Fig. 5.4(a)).

- Let ex_0 be the partial execution in which all processes in the system crash at the beginning of the execution except processes from Q_1. Moreover, in ex_1, p_1 invokes $write(v)$. Due to our assumption on I and since there is a quorum that contains only correct processes (Q_1), $write(v)$ eventually completes in ex_1. Moreover, the latency of $write(v)$ is at most two message delays, i.e., processes from Q_1 receive the message from p_1 and reply to p_1 (we refer to a round). We collectively refer to the state of processes from $B_2 \subseteq Q_1$, after every process from B_2 receives the message from p_1, as to st_0.

[3]The rest of the proof is virtually the same in case we select p_1 and/or p_2 to be outside $Q_1 \cup Q_2$.

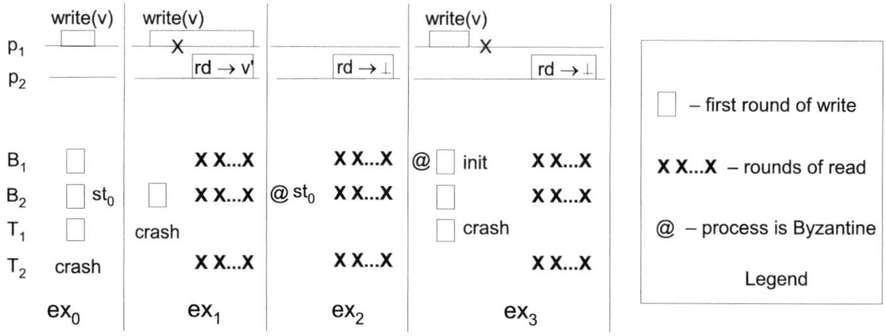

(a) *write* lower bound executions

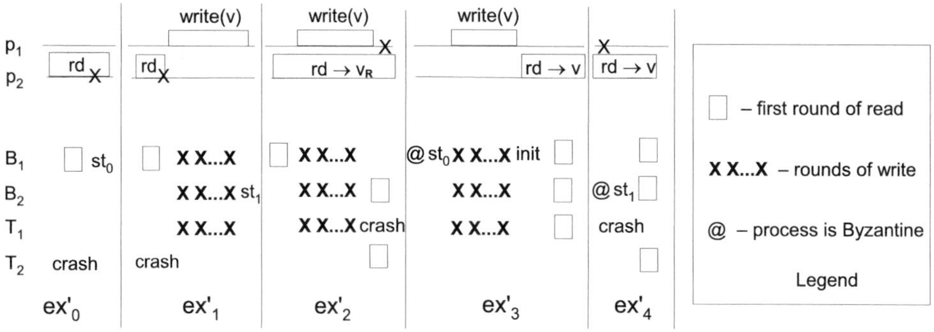

(b) *read* lower bound executions

Figure 5.4: Executions illustrating the proof of Theorem 5.24.

- Let ex_1 be a different partial execution in which all processes in the system crash at the beginning of the execution except processes from $Q_2 \cup \{p_1\}$. In ex_1, p_1 invokes $write(v)$ and then crashes, such that only processes from B_2 receive the message from p_1; hence, the state of processes from B_2 is st_0 (see ex_0). Then, in ex_1, p_2 invokes $read()$. Due to our assumption on I and since there is a quorum that contains only correct processes (Q_2), $read$ by p_2 eventually completes in ex_1. By definition of the safe register $read$ by p_2 returns some value v'.

- Let ex_2 be a partial execution similar to ex_1 in which all processes in the system crash at the beginning of the execution except processes from Q_2. Moreover, processes in B_2 are Byzantine and switch their state to st_0 at the beginning of the execution. Afterwards, processes from B_2 send exactly the same messages as in ex_1. Then, in ex_2, p_2 invokes $read()$. Since p_2 cannot distinguish ex_2 from ex_1, $read()$ eventually completes in ex_2 and returns v'. However, by definition of the safe register $read$ must return $\perp$ in ex_2 (since no $write$ was invoked) and, hence $v' = \perp$.

- Finally, let ex_3 be an execution similar to ex_0 in which, at the beginning, only processes from $Q_1 \cup Q_2$ are correct, the rest being crash faulty. In ex_3, p_1 invokes $write(v)$ just like in ex_0; however processes from $Q_2 \setminus Q_1$ never receive any message from p_1 (due to asynchrony). Since p_1 cannot distinguish ex_3 from ex_0, $write(v)$ completes in ex_3 just like in ex_0. After completion of $write$: (1) processes from $Q_1 \setminus Q_2$ (including p_1) fail by crashing, and (2) processes from B_1 fail Byzantine, and switch their state to the initial state. Hence, only processes from $Q_2 \setminus B_1$, including those from B_2 are correct. Process $p_2 \in Q_2$ then invokes (read). Notice that p_2 cannot distinguish ex_3 from ex_1 since only processes from Q_2 that have state different from the initial one are processes from B_2. Hence, (read) eventually completes in ex_3 and p_2 returns v'. However, $v' = \perp$ (see ex_2). This violates safeness consistency semantics, since in ex_3, $write(v)$ precedes $read$, which must return v.

Now assume by contradiction that a SWSR storage implementation I in which the worst-case latency of $read$ is two message delays exists (illustrations are given in Fig. 5.4(b)).

- Let ex'_0 be the partial execution in which all process crash at the beginning of the execution, except those from $Q_1 \cup \{p_2\}$. In ex'_0, p_2 invokes $read$ and no other operation is invoked in ex'_0. Besides, in ex'_0, p_2 crashes and its messages reach only processes from B_1 such that p_2 receives no replies. After processes B_1 send replies to p_2, ex'_0 ends. We collectively refer to the state of processes from B_1, at the end of ex'_0 as to st_0.

- Let ex'_1 be an execution that extends ex'_0 by appending a $write(v)$ operation by p_1. Since there is a quorum containing correct processes in ex'_1 (Q_1), $write(v)$ completes in $ex'1$, when the partial execution ends (at time t_1). We refer to the state of the processes from B_2 at the end of ex'_1 as to st_1.

- Let ex'_2 be the partial execution identical to ex'_1 up to t_1, except that: (1) processes from $Q_2 \setminus Q_1$ do not crash but (i) due to asynchrony processes from $Q_2 \setminus Q_1$ do not receive any message in ex'_2; except, (ii) messages from reader p_2 which are received by processes from $Q_2 \setminus Q_1$ after t_1, and (2) processes from $Q_1 \setminus Q_2$ crash at time t_1.

  Since the writer p_1 cannot distinguish ex'_2 from ex'_1, $write(v)$ completes in $ex'1$ at time t_1 (just before p_1 crashes). Moreover, since there is a quorum of correct processes in ex'_2 (Q_2), $read$ eventually completes in ex'_2, at time t_2, when ex'_2 ends. Moreover, the latency of $read$ is at most two message delays, i.e., processes from Q_2 receive the message from p_2 and reply to p_2. We denote the value returned by the $read$ in ex'_2 by v_R.

- Let ex'_3 be the partial run similar to ex'_2, except that, in ex'_3: (1) p_2 invokes $read$ only after $write(v)$ completes (i.e., after t_1); (2) processes from B_1 are Byzantine and change their state to st_0 at the beginning of ex'_3 (as if they received a $read$ message from the reader p_2, as in ex'_2); (3) at t_1, B_1, before sending any message to processes from Q_2, changes again its state to the initial state. Otherwise, in ex'_3, messages are delivered as in ex'_2. Notice that neither p_1 nor p_2 can distinguish ex'_3 from ex'_2; hence, $write(v)$ (resp., $read$) completes in ex'_3 at t_1 (resp., t_2). Moreover, $read$ returns the same value as in ex'_2, i.e., v_R. However, since $read$ is invoked in ex'_3 after completion of $write(v)$, by safeness, $v_R = v$.

- Finally, consider the partial execution ex'_4 in which only $write$ is never invoked, but processes from B_2 are Byzantine and change their state to st_1 (see ex'_1) at the beginning of the execution. The processes from $Q_2 \setminus B_2$ are correct, and processes outside Q_2 fail by crashing at the beginning of ex'_4. In ex'_4, p_2 invokes $read$. Processes from Q_2 receive the message from p_2 and send the reply to p_2. When p_2 receives the replies from all processes from Q_2, $read$ must complete, since p_2 and other correct objects from $Q_2 \setminus B_2$, cannot distinguish ex'_4 from ex'_3. Hence, in ex'_4, $read$ returns $v_R = v \neq \perp$, a value that was never written, instead of $\perp$ as stipulated by safeness. A contradiction.

□

5.2.2 STORAGE EMULATION

As we already mentioned, masking quorum systems were initially proposed as quorum systems to be used when storing data in the unauthenticated Byzantine fault model. Here, we present an algorithm, simply called MR [Malkhi and Reiter, 1998a], which emulates a single-writer multi-reader (SWMR) safe storage emulation in the unauthenticated model.

Like Phalanx (Sec. 5.1.2), MR is again very similar to ABD (Sec. 4.1), except that it makes use of a masking quorum system $\boldsymbol{MQS}$ over a set of servers and does not use digital signatures which are disallowed in the unauthenticated model. Moreover, since it implements only safe consistency semantics, MR does not require the neither the Timestamp synchronization phase, nor the Writeback phase. Hence, in MR, both $read$ and $write$ operations require one access to a quorum, i.e., the worst case latency of MR is 2 message delays. Hence, MR complements Theorem 5.6 by exhibiting the sufficient part for the existence of single-round storage emulations in the unauthenticated Byzantine fault model. MR tolerates Byzantine readers by construction, since the $read$ operation does not modify the state of a server. Moreover, MR tolerates crash-faulty writers.

The client pseudocode of MR is given in Algorithm 21. It is very similar to the client pseudocode of ABD (Algorithm 3), stripped of the Timestamp synchronization and Writeback phases and with the modified Read phase. The $write$ pseudocode of MR is derived in a straightforward manner from the ABD Write phase, by eliminating writer IDs from $write$ messages and by overloading operation counter $opCnt$ to serve as a timestamp as well.

The server pseudocode is given in Algorithm 22; it is a straightforward simplification of the server code of ABD (Algorithm 4) applicable in the single writer context.

Algorithm 21 MR algorithm (client c pseudocode)

Local variables initialization: $opCnt \leftarrow 0; maxval \leftarrow \perp$

1: **upon** $inv_c(MR, write(v))$ **do**
2:     $opCnt \leftarrow opCnt + 1$
3:     $send\ (write, v, opCnt)$ to all servers
4:     **when** $receive\ (writeack, opCnt)$ from all s_i from some $Q \in MQS$
5:         **return** $resp_c(MR, ack)$
6:     **end when**
7: **end upon**

8: **upon** $inv_c(MR, read())$ **do**
9:     $opCnt \leftarrow opCnt + 1$
10:    $send\ (read, opCnt)$ to all servers
11:    **when** $receive\ m_i = (readack, val_i, ts_i, opCnt)$ from all s_i from some $Q \in MQS$
12:        $recPairs \leftarrow \{\langle ts, val \rangle | \exists R \subseteq Q, \forall s_i \in R : R \notin B \land m_i.val_i = val \land m_i.ts_i = ts\}$
13:        **if** $recPairs \neq \emptyset$ **then**
14:            $maxval \leftarrow val$ with maximum timestamp ts such that $\langle ts, val \rangle \in recPairs$
15:            **return** $resp_c(MR, maxval)$
16:        **else**
17:            **return** $resp_c(MR, \perp)$
18:        **end if**
19:    **end when**
20: **end upon**

Algorithm 22 MR algorithm (server s_i pseudocode)

Local variables initialization: $ts_i = 0; val_i \leftarrow \perp$

upon $receive\ (read, cnt)$ from client c **do**
    $send(readack, val_i, ts_i, cnt)$ to c
end upon
upon $receive\ (write, val', cnt)$ from client c **do**
    if $cnt > ts_i$ **then**
        $ts_i \leftarrow cnt; val_i \leftarrow val'$
    end if
    $send(writeack, cnt)$ to c
end upon

The key idea in MR *read* implementation is that it relies on the M-Byzantine intersection property of masking quorum systems; this is captured by the way a reader returns a value after it collects responses from a quorum Q of servers (lines 12-18, Algorithm 21). A reader cannot select the value with a highest timestamp (like in ABD) since, in the unauthenticated model, a Byzantine server can easily forge a value with a highest timestamp and compromise consistency of a *read*. MR implements safe semantics, therefore we focus solely on the case where a *read* is uncontented, i.e., not overlapping any *write* operation.

First, in line 12, the reader extracts all the timestamp-value pairs $\langle ts, val \rangle$ that have been reported in *readack* messages from a subset R of Q such that, R does not belong to the adversary. This guarantees that $\langle ts, val \rangle$ is reported by at least one benign server, which in turn implies that the value was indeed written by a writer. Out of these timestamp-value pairs, a reader selects the one with the highest timestamp (line 14, Algorithm 21) and returns this value. However, in case there is no such a timestamp-value pair, a reader returns a default value $\perp$, which indicates a *read* concurrent with a *write* (line 17, Algorithm 21).

Lemma 5.25 *The MR algorithm satisfies safeness in every execution.*

Proof. *Sketch.* To prove the lemma, it is sufficient to show that, in MR, an uncontended *read* rd returns the value val written by the last *write* that precedes rd. By Definition 2.12, if there is no invoked *write* wr that precedes rd, the initial *write* is the last preceding *write* for rd and rd returns $\perp$.

To see this, notice that the writer writes val with timestamp ts in a masking quorum Q of servers (this holds for the initial *write* as well). Later, a reader accesses a quorum Q' of servers and obtains the timestamp-value pairs. Since Q' might include a set B of Byzantine servers, only $(Q \cap Q') \setminus B$ correct servers are guaranteed to report val in rd. However, by Def. 5.18, $(Q \cap Q') \setminus B \notin \mathbf{B}$. Hence, $\langle ts, val \rangle \in recPairs$ in line 12 (Algorithm 21). By our assumption on wr, ts is the highest timestamp in $recPairs$ since servers from B cannot forge a value that will be included in $recPairs$. Therefore, rd returns val. □

Remark 5.26 Unlike in ABD and Phalanx, in MR a reader cannot writeback the value val selected to obtain atomic semantics. The reason is clearly a possible return of $\perp$ in case of a *read* concurrent with a *write*. The writeback technique is only useful to make a regular emulation atomic, whereas MR implements safe semantics only.

Notice also that the use of masking quorum systems in MR implies the knowledge of the adversary (see line 12, Algorithm 21). In the following section, we discuss a variant of masking quorum systems, called *opaque* quorum systems where the client of a quorum system does not need to know its adversary.

5.3 OPAQUE QUORUM SYSTEMS

5.3.1 BASICS

Opaque quorum systems [Malkhi and Reiter, 1998a] are a specific variant of masking quorum systems designed for the case where the adversary is *opaque*. Here, the notion of opacity implies that the adversary is fixed, yet not known to correct processes. Roughly speaking, this quorum system provides an invariant stating that the *count* on the number of correct processes in an intersection of any two quorums will be higher (or equal) to the number of stale processes in any given quorum plus the number of Byzantine processes.

More specifically, when a writer writes in a quorum Q and the reader reads from a quorum Q', with set B containing Byzantine processes, opaque quorum systems guarantee that the *number* of benign processes in $Q' \cap Q$ will be greater (or equal) to the sum of the total number of stale processes in Q', i.e., $|Q' \setminus Q|$, and the number of Byzantine processes in Q', which is at most $|Q' \cap B|$ (see Fig. 5.5). This guarantees that the latest written value with outnumber a stale value (equality is allowed in case timestamps are used). Moreover, the *number* of benign processes in $Q' \cap Q$ must be strictly greater than the number of Byzantine processes in Q' so that a valid value can outnumber the value possibly forged by Byzantine processes. This leads us to the definition of opaque quorum systems.

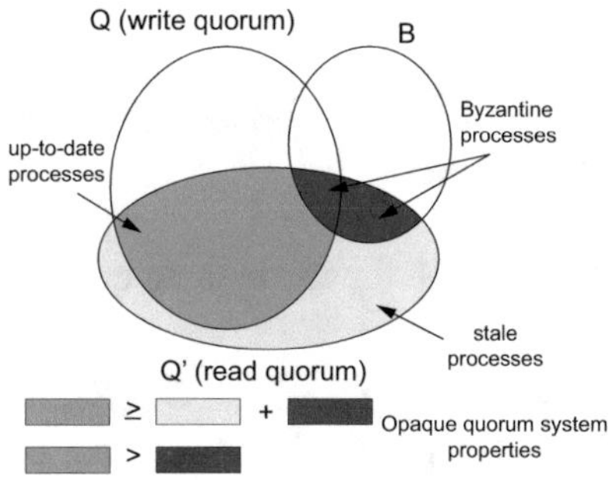

Figure 5.5: Intersection properties of opaque quorum systems.

Definition 5.27 Opaque quorum systems Given a set S and an adversary $\boldsymbol{B}$ for S, a quorum system (over S) $\boldsymbol{OQS}$ is an opaque quorum system over S if and only if

(O-Stale consistency) $\forall Q_1, Q_2 \in \boldsymbol{OQS}, \forall B \in \boldsymbol{B} : |(Q_1 \cap Q_2) \setminus B| \geq |(Q_2 \setminus Q_1) \cup (Q_2 \cap B)|$
(O-Byzantine consistency) $\forall Q_1, Q_2 \in \boldsymbol{OQS}, \forall B \in \boldsymbol{B} : |(Q_1 \cap Q_2) \setminus B| > |Q_2 \cap B|$.

Analogously to $t-$dissemination and $t-$masking quorum systems, we define $t-$opaque quorum systems.

Definition 5.28 ***t*−opaque quorum systems** Given the adversary $\boldsymbol{B}_t$, an opaque quorum system is a t-opaque quorum system if its resilience is at least t.

Theorem 5.29 Lower bound No t-resilient opaque quorum systems can be constructed with less than $5t$ processes.

Proof. Consider any $t-$dissemination quorum system $\boldsymbol{tOQS}$. Then, by Definition 3.22, there are two quorums $Q_1, Q_2 \in \boldsymbol{tOQS}$ such that $Q_1 \leq n-t$ and $Q_2 \leq n-t$, such that $Q_2 \setminus Q_1 = t$. Therefore, $|Q_1 \cap Q_2| \leq n-2t$.

On the other hand, by O-Byzantine consistency for all $B \in \boldsymbol{B}$ $|(Q_1 \cap Q_2) \setminus B| > 0$, i.e., $\exists B_1 \in \boldsymbol{B}$ such that $|B_1| = t$ and $B_1 \in Q_1 \cap Q_2$. Hence, $|(Q_1 \cap Q_2) \setminus B| \leq n-3t$.

Applying O-Stale consistency, we have $|(Q_2 \setminus Q_1) \cup (Q_2 \cap B_1)| \leq n-3t$. However,

$$|(Q_2 \setminus Q_1) \cup (Q_2 \cap B_1)| \overset{B_1 \subseteq Q_2}{=} |(Q_2 \setminus Q_1)| + |B_1| = t + t = 2t \ .$$

Hence, $n \geq 5t$. □

Opaque quorum systems have higher load than dissemination and masking quorum systems, as captured by the following Theorem.

Theorem 5.30 Load $\mathcal{L}(\boldsymbol{OQS}) \geq \frac{1}{2}$ for any opaque quorum system $\boldsymbol{OQS}$.

Proof. By O-Stale consistency for any $Q_1, Q_2 \in \boldsymbol{OQS}$, we have $|(Q_1 \cap Q_2)| \geq |(Q_1 \setminus Q_2) = |Q_1| - |Q_1 \cap Q_2|$, which implies $|(Q_1 \cap Q_2)| \geq \frac{|Q_1|}{2}$. Let σ be any strategy and fix any $Q_i \in \boldsymbol{OQS}$.

$$\sum_{s_i \in Q_i} l_\sigma(s_i, \boldsymbol{OQS}) \overset{\text{Def. 3.11}}{=} \sum_{s_i \in Q_i} \sum_{Q \ni s_i} \sigma_{\boldsymbol{OQS}}(Q)$$

$$= \sum_{Q} \sum_{s_i \in Q \cap Q_i} \sigma_{\boldsymbol{OQS}}(Q) \geq \sum_{Q} \frac{|Q_i|}{2} \sigma_{\boldsymbol{OQS}}(Q) = \frac{|Q_i|}{2}$$

which implies that at least one element of Q_i suffers the load of at least $\frac{1}{2}$.

□

5.3.2 STORAGE EMULATION

The MR emulation (Sec. 5.2.2) that relies on masking quorum systems with the knowledge of the adversary can be simply modified to relax the assumption on the knowledge of the adversary with an opaque quorum system replacing the masking one. The resulting emulation [Malkhi and Reiter, 1998a], that we simply refer to as MR2, also implements a single-writer multi-reader safe storage emulation in the unauthenticated model.

To obtain MR2 from MR, we replace the lines 11-19 in Algorithm 21, with the code given in Algorithm 23. We also need to replace the masking quorum systems with an opaque one.

Algorithm 23 MR2 algorithm (excerpt of the client c pseudocode)

upon $receive\ (readack, val_i, ts_i, c_i, opCnt)$ from all s_i from some $Q \in \boldsymbol{OQS}$ **do**
  $mostFrequentPairs \leftarrow \{\langle ts_i, val_i \rangle\}$ such that the pair $\langle ts_i, val_i \rangle$ appears most often in received $readack$ messages
  $maxval \leftarrow val$ with maximum timestamp ts such that $\langle ts, val \rangle \in mostFrequentPairs$
  return $resp_c(MR2, maxval)$
end upon

Clearly, MR2 abolishes the requirement for knowing the adversary $\boldsymbol{B}$ because it uses opaque quorum systems instead of masking ones. Indeed, notice that Algorithm 23 does not assume that the client knows $\boldsymbol{B}$. Proving the correctness (i.e., safeness) of MR2 is rather straightforward.

It is interesting to observe that the use of timestamps can be fairly simply removed from MR2, if an opaque quorum system with strict inequality in O-Stale consistency is used. The resulting algorithm, called JCT [Jayanti et al., 1998], is given in Algorithm 24.

Besides the absence of timestamps, JCT is different from MR2 since JCT is an implementation in the shared memory model. More specifically, JCT is a fault-tolerant implementation of a safe SWMR register out of a set $\mathcal{R}$ of fault-prone base SWMR register,[4] numbered from $1 \ldots |\mathcal{R}|$ over which an opaque quorum system (with strict O-Stale inequality) $\boldsymbol{sOQS}$ is formed. The proof of JCT (as well as of MR2) is rather straightforward and is left as an exercise.

5.4 BIBLIOGRAPHIC NOTES

- Although it has been known for some time that tolerating Byzantine failures in, e.g., consensus requires a larger fraction of correct processes than tolerating crash failures only does (e.g., the seminal work [Lamport et al., 1982a]), the first formal treatment of the problem of defining quorum systems in Byzantine context was done in [Malkhi and Reiter, 1998a]. [Malkhi and Reiter, 1998a] was the work that defined three classes of Byzantine quorum systems that we described: dissemination, masking and opaque quorum systems.

[4]Such implementations of a shared object O using several fault-prone copies of O are called *self-implementations*.

Algorithm 24 JCT algorithm

Local variables initialization:
$invoked \leftarrow \emptyset; responded \leftarrow \emptyset; val \leftarrow \perp; pending \leftarrow \emptyset \ i \leftarrow 0 \ responses \leftarrow \emptyset$ (a multiset)

1: **upon** base register j responds with response val_j **and** $j \in pending$ **do**
2:    **if** $j \in invoked$ **then**
3:      $responses \leftarrow responses \cup \{val_j\}$
4:      $responded \leftarrow responded \cup \{j\}$
5:    **end if**
6:    $pending \leftarrow pending \setminus \{j\}$
7: **end upon**
8: **upon** $inv_c(JCT, write(v))$ **or** $inv_c(JCT, read())$ **do**
9:    $invoked \leftarrow \emptyset$
10:   $responses \leftarrow \emptyset$
11:   $responded \leftarrow \emptyset$
12:   $i \leftarrow 0$
13:   **repeat**
14:     $i \leftarrow i \bmod \mathcal{R} + 1$
15:     **if** $i \notin pending$ **and** $i \notin invoked$ **then**
16:       **if** $write$ operation is invoked **then**
17:         $inv_c(i, write(v))$
18:       **else**   {Read operation}
19:         $inv_c(i, read())$
20:       **end if**
21:       $invoked \leftarrow invoked \cup \{i\}$
22:       $pending \leftarrow pending \cup \{i\}$
23:     **end if**
24:   **until** $responded \in sOQS$
25:   **if** $write$ operation is invoked **then**
26:     **return** $resp_c(JCT, ack)$
27:   **else**   {Read operation}
28:     $val \leftarrow$ value that appears most often in $responses$
29:     **return** $resp_c(JCT, val)$
30:   **end if**
31: **end upon**

- The load and availability of Byzantine quorum systems was first studied in [Malkhi et al., 2000].

- Dissemination quorum systems, in particular $\mathbf{Maj}_{\frac{2}{3}}$ (assuming $\mathbf{B}_{\lfloor\frac{n-1}{3}\rfloor}$), underlie many other Byzantine fault-tolerant protocols beyond storage, including replication protocols. Examples include the seminal work of [Castro and Liskov, 2002], or the replication protocols of [Cowling et al., 2006].

- In [Malkhi and Reiter, 1998a], a single-writer multi-reader regular storage construction for storing authenticated data using dissemination quorum systems in which both reads and writes access a given quorum only once. This approach was further extended in [Malkhi and Reiter, 1998b] to implement multi-writer multi-reader atomic storage relying again on dissemination quorum systems and digital signatures (Phalanx algorithm, given in Sec. 5.1.2). Just like with crash faults, the improvement in terms of supporting multiple writers and providing stronger semantics came at the price of having to access quorums twice in each read and write.

- [Martin et al., 2002a] proposed asymmetric variants of dissemination and masking quorum systems that account for the distinction between read and write quorums. The same work also proposed the construction of threshold-based disseminating and masking quorum systems with as few as $2t + 1$ and $3t + 1$ processes, respectively. To achieve this, these quorum systems sacrifice the resilience of write quorums but maintain read quorums t-resilient.

- Masking quorum systems were used in the atomic storage construction of [Bazzi and Ding, 2004] and the regular one of [Abraham et al., 2007]. A variation of masking quorum systems in the synchronous model was used in [Bazzi, 2000b].

- The first atomic storage emulation that stores unauthenticated data using only dissemination quorums was shown in [Martin et al., 2002b]. Not surprisingly, this protocol called SBQ-L (Small Byzantine Quorums with Listeners), used much more involved techniques than the Phalanx protocol of [Malkhi and Reiter, 1998b]. Using masking quorums helps achieve simpler design (e.g., the MR protocol), but it comes with the price of lower resilience and higher load, as we already discussed.

- CL algorithm first appeared in the context of the PBFT replication protocol [Castro and Liskov, 2002]. The variant given here is the adaptation of the modular consensus algorithm presented in [Guerraoui and Vukolić, 2010].

- Following the work of [Martin et al., 2002b], many storage constructions that use disseminating quorum systems to store unauthenticated data were proposed, typically with the goal of reducing complexity. These include safe and regular storage constructions of [Abraham et al., 2006] and [Guerraoui and Vukolić, 2006], as well as the atomic storage construction of [Aiyer et al., 2007].

- Our Theorem 5.24, which implies that any consistent (i.e., safe) storage that stores unauthenticated data in a disseminating, non-masking, quorum must have *write* and *read* operations access a quorum more than once in the worst case, was first shown in the case of the threshold adversary in [Abraham et al., 2006] (for *write*) and in [Abraham et al., 2006, Guerraoui and Vukolić, 2006] (for *read*).

- [Bazzi, 2001] also extends the notion of Byzantine quorum systems, defining *non-blocking* quorum systems in the context of studying the asynchronous access cost of quorum systems.

CHAPTER 6

Latency-efficient Quorum Systems

6.1 INTRODUCTION

A lot of attention in distributed computing is focused on optimizing common-case system behavior. The typical research goal in this context is to provide reliable, robust and consistent service under worst-case system conditions, i.e., asynchrony, large number of failures and high concurrency, and at the same time have such a service perform efficiently in the common-case, characterized by synchrony, few faults, and possibly even low concurrency. Distributed protocols proposed in this context include, for example: (i) replication protocols, both crash-tolerant ones such as Fast Paxos [Lamport, 2006] and Byzantine fault-tolerant ones such as Q/U [Abd-El-Malek et al., 2005], Zyzzyva [Kotla et al., 2009] or Aliph [Guerraoui et al., 2010]; (ii) atomic read/write storage protocols of [Goodson et al., 2004] and [Guerraoui et al., 2006]; (iii) consensus protocols of [Martin and Alvisi, 2006] and [Zielinski, 2006]; and (iv) the atomic broadcast protocol of [Ramasamy and Cachin, 2005]. A typical goal of such protocols is to minimize the common-case latency, i.e., the number of quorum accesses in the common case. We collectively refer to these protocols as *fast* protocols.

Ideally, a given quorum should be accessed only once (such as in a single-round emulation, Sec. 5.2.2) in particular in the common case. However, and as we already discussed, this is not the case even for a relatively simple crash-tolerant atomic storage emulation such as ABD (Sec. 4.1). Recall that in ABD even the *read* operation needs to access quorums twice first in its Read phase and then in the Writeback phase. Similarly, in Paxos/Synod consensus algorithm (Sec. 4.2), two quorum accesses are needed, boiling down to 4 message delays, with an additional message delay related to proposer sending a message to the leader, thus totalling 5 message delays. However, in the common-case we would expect the best possible latency, e.g., one quorum access in ABD and Paxos/Synod, corresponding to two message delays. In principle, fast protocols precisely target this, optimal latency.

It turns out that fast protocols, in particular those that target optimal resilience, rely in the worst case on classical (e.g., majorities) and dissemination quorum systems (e.g., $\mathbf{Maj}_{\frac{2}{3}}$). However, in the common case, these protocols typically require quorums that are to be accessed only once to have *larger* intersections with other quorums to maintain consistency. The size of such *fast*, or *latency-efficient* quorums, depends on the desired consistency semantics. In general, the nature of such larger quorum intersections is not captured by classical, dissemination or even masking quorum systems.

Namely, these quorum systems, that we covered in Chapters 3 and 5 might be necessary and/or sufficient for fast implementations in certain cases. For example, classical and dissemination quorum systems are necessary and sufficient for fast implementations of SWMR regular storage in the crash-fault and authenticated Byzantine fault-model respectively, as we discussed in Secs. 4.1 and 5.1.2. Moreover, masking quorum systems are sufficient for fast, single-round SWMR safe storage in the unauthenticated Byzantine fault model, as exemplified by the MR storage protocol in Sec. 5.2.2. However, they are not sufficient for fast implementations of the strongest consistency semantics, linearizability or atomicity, which is needed for atomic storage and consensus. Hence, the general characterization that would capture both the necessary and sufficient conditions for fast quorums must involve an interplay between three different parameters: (1) consistency semantics type, (2) type of faults tolerated (crash vs. Byzantine), and (3) (in case of Byzantine faults) authentication.

In this chapter, we describe further refinement of classical and Byzantine quorum systems called *refined quorum systems* [Guerraoui and Vukolić, 2010], which provides such a general characterization of fast quorums. Unlike a classical or a Byzantine quorum systems, a refined quorum system is a hierarchical one.

Namely, refined quorum systems refine distinguish *three different quorum classes*. The use of these three classes of refined quorum systems is intuitive: to obtain the strongest, atomic, semantics, in the common case, a distributed storage or consensus implementation can expedite an operation accessing a first-class quorum by allowing it to access such a quorum only once, whereas quorums of the second and the third class must be accessed at least twice and three times, respectively. Refined quorum systems are designed for use both in the Byzantine fault model and in the simple crash fault model.

We further exemplify refined quorum systems by discussing two distributed emulations: the consensus algorithm of the Fast Paxos replication protocol [Lamport, 2006] in Sec. 6.3.1 and the SWMR atomic storage emulation of [Guerraoui and Vukolić, 2010], here referred to as GV, in Sec. 6.3.2.

6.2 REFINED QUORUM SYSTEMS

6.2.1 BASICS

Refined quorum systems are defined as follows.

Definition 6.1 Refined quorum systems Given a set S, a dissemination quorum system $\boldsymbol{RQS}$ with adversary $\boldsymbol{B}$ for S, and two set systems $\boldsymbol{QC_1}$ and $\boldsymbol{QC_2}$ over S, a triple $(\boldsymbol{QC_1}, \boldsymbol{QC_2}, \boldsymbol{RQS})$ is a refined quorum system over S,[1] if and only if $\boldsymbol{QC_1} \subseteq \boldsymbol{QC_2} \subseteq \boldsymbol{RQS}$ and

(Class-1 inters.) $\forall Q_1, Q_1' \in \boldsymbol{QC_1}, \forall Q \in \boldsymbol{RQS}, \forall B_1, B_2 \in \boldsymbol{B} : Q_1 \cap Q_1' \cap Q \not\subseteq B_1 \cup B_2$, and

[1]We sometimes simply say $\boldsymbol{RQS}$ is a refined quorum system if $\boldsymbol{QC_1}$ and $\boldsymbol{QC_2}$ are evident from the context.

(Class-2 inters.) $\forall Q_1 \in \boldsymbol{QC_1}, \forall Q_2 \in \boldsymbol{QC_2}, \forall Q \in \boldsymbol{RQS}, \forall B_1, B_2 \in \boldsymbol{B}$:

$$(Q_2 \cap Q \not\subseteq B_1 \cup B_2) \bigvee (\boldsymbol{QC_1} \neq \emptyset \wedge Q_1 \cap Q_2 \cap Q \not\subseteq B_1).$$

Remark 6.2 Notice that Definition 6.1 defines refined quorum systems as a special case of dissemination quorum systems, which implies that Byzantine intersection property (Def. 5.4) holds for $\boldsymbol{RQS}$, i.e.,

(Byzantine intersection) $\forall Q, Q' \in \mathbf{RQS}, \forall B \in \mathbf{B} : Q \cap Q' \not\subseteq B$.

In the context of refined quorum systems we sometimes refer to the Byzantine intersection property as to Class-3 intersection property.

Notation 6.3

1. Quorums that belong to $\boldsymbol{QC_1}$ are called *class 1* quorums.
2. Quorums that belong to $\boldsymbol{QC_2} \setminus \boldsymbol{QC_1}$ are called *class 2* quorums.
3. The remaining quorums that belong to $\boldsymbol{RQS} \setminus \boldsymbol{QC_2}$ are called *class 3* quorums.

Notation 6.4 Given a refined quorum system $(\boldsymbol{QC_1}, \boldsymbol{QC_2}, \boldsymbol{RQS})$, such that $\boldsymbol{QC_1} \neq \emptyset$ fix $Q_2 \in \boldsymbol{QC_2}$, $Q \in \boldsymbol{RQS}$ and $B \in \boldsymbol{B}$ to define the following predicates:

$C_{2a}(Q_2, Q, B) \stackrel{\text{def}}{=} \forall B' \in \boldsymbol{B} : Q_2 \cap Q \notin B \cup B'$, and
$C_{2b}(Q_2, Q, B) \stackrel{\text{def}}{=} \forall Q_1 \in \boldsymbol{QC_1} : Q_1 \cap Q_2 \cap Q \not\subseteq B$.

The following Lemma follows directly from the Class-2 intersection property of Definition 6.1.

Lemma 6.5 *Given a refined quorum system* $(\boldsymbol{QC_1}, \boldsymbol{QC_2}, \boldsymbol{RQS})$ *over adversary* $\boldsymbol{B}$, $\forall Q_2 \in \boldsymbol{QC_2}, \forall Q \in \boldsymbol{RQS}, \forall B \in \boldsymbol{B} : C_{2a}(Q_2, Q, B) \vee C_{2b}(Q_2, Q, B)$.

Finally, we define a special, yet important family of refined quorum systems, in which all quorums belong to the first class.

Definition 6.6 Uniform refined quorum systems A refined quorum system $(\boldsymbol{QC_1}, \boldsymbol{QC_2}, \boldsymbol{RQS})$ is called *uniform* if $\boldsymbol{QC_1} = \boldsymbol{QC_2} = \boldsymbol{RQS}$.

6.2.2 INTUITION

In their most general form stipulated by Definition 6.1, refined quorum systems are designed with providing atomic semantics in the unauthenticated Byzantine fault model in mind. In this context, refined quorum systems provide necessary and sufficient conditions for fast and *gracefully degrading* storage and consensus protocols with the following behavior: when a class 1 quorum is available a protocol requires such a quorum to be accessed only once in the common case (recall that in the case of storage this subsumes synchrony and an uncontended operation). Otherwise, the protocols gracefully degrade to require 2 (resp., 3) accesses in case a class 2 (resp., 3) quorum is available. This hierarchy among quorums obtains a simple form when the requirement for atomic semantics, tolerating Byzantine faults and/or no authentication is relaxed. We discuss these simplifications later; first we give the intuition behind full blown refined quorums.

The intuition behind the Class-1 intersection property can roughly be summarized in the requirement that the intersection X between any two class 1 quorums Q_1 and Q'_1, respectively, accessed only once by e.g., the writer and the reader, must have enough information for a subsequent reader accessing some quorum Q, so that the latter does not return the stale value or a value forged by Byzantine processes (see Fig. 6.1). Intuitively, X (where $X = Q_1 \cap Q'_1$) and Q should intersect here just like masking quorums do since data is not authenticated.

The intuition behind the Class-2 intersection property is more involved: we explain it here assuming a write accessing a class 1 quorum Q_1 and a read rd that accesses a class 2 quorum Q_2, followed by another read rd' that accesses some class 3 quorum Q (see Fig. 6.2 for an illustration assuming threshold adversary $\boldsymbol{B}_1$). The key idea here is that rd is allowed to access class 2 quorum Q_2 twice. Moreover, in the common case, the reader will know which value it should return already after the first access of Q_2. Then, in the second access, the reader can "confirm" the value by writing it back to quorum Q_2. In case Q_2 has a masking-like intersection with class 3 quorums, including Q (see the first condition in the disjunction), this is sufficient for rd' not to miss the value read by rd. On the other hand, such a masking-like quorum intersection of class 2 quorums is not always necessary. Namely (see the second condition in the disjunction), if intersections between class 1 quorums and Q_2 act like dissemination quorums with respect to class 3 quorums, it is sufficient that the reader "authenticates" the data by writing the value for the second time in the intersection $X = Q_1 \cap Q_2$ when it accesses Q_2 for the second time. Here, roughly speaking, writing the value in nodes in X (at least) twice (once by the writer and once by the reader) has the effect of strengthening and confirming unauthenticated data so the masking intersection is no longer required. We further elaborate the Class-2 intersection property in Sec. 6.2.3.

6.2.3 EXAMPLES

Crash faults. The special case of a refined quorum systems is obtained by letting $\boldsymbol{B} = \{\emptyset\}$ — this gives us a latency-efficient quorum system to be used in crash-fault tolerant atomic storage and consensus emulations. In the case $\boldsymbol{B} = \{\emptyset\}$, Class-3 intersection property implies Class-2 intersection property; notice that this further implies that in the crash case there are no class 3 quorums, but only

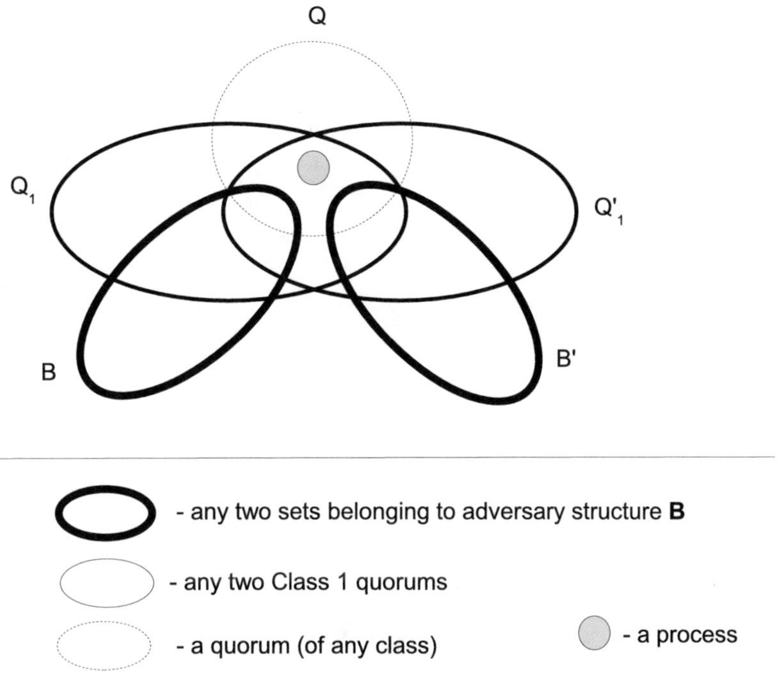

Figure 6.1: Class-1 intersection property: For any two class 1 quorums Q_1 and Q'_1, any quorum Q and any two elements of the adversary B and B', it is critical that $(Q_1 \cap Q'_1 \cap Q) \setminus (B \cup B')$ contains at least one process.

class 2 and class 1 quorums. Moreover, the Class-3 intersection property becomes itself the classical one. Hence, a refined quorum system given $\boldsymbol{B} = \{\emptyset\}$, is any quorum system $\boldsymbol{QS}$ with $\boldsymbol{QC_1} \subseteq \boldsymbol{QS}$ such that

$$\forall Q_1, Q'_1 \in \boldsymbol{QC_1}, \forall Q \in \boldsymbol{QS} : Q_1 \cap Q'_1 \cap Q \neq \emptyset.$$

Put differently, $(\boldsymbol{QC_1}, \boldsymbol{QS}, \boldsymbol{QS})$ is a refined quorum system for $\boldsymbol{B} = \{\emptyset\}$. Such a refined quorum system has been implicitly used in many fast protocols in the crash-fault model, notably in the consensus algorithm of the Fast Paxos replication protocol [Lamport, 2006], that we describe in Sec. 6.3.1.

Non-atomic semantics. As we intuited in Sec. 6.2.2, Class-1 intersection property is critical for achieving fast storage and replication protocols that require linearizable, or atomic semantics. However, and as we saw on the example of MR algorithm 5.2.2, Class 1 intersection property is not needed for non-atomic, e.g., safe semantics. It turns out that for non-atomic semantics, the variant

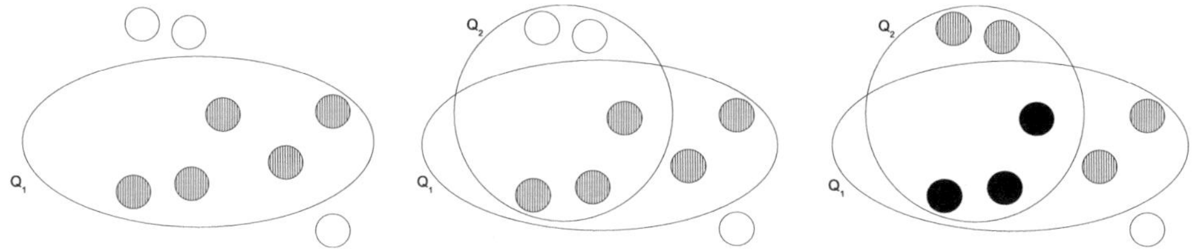

(a) A *write* writes unauthenticated data into a class 1 quorum Q_1

(b) A subsequent *read rd* accesses class 2 quorum Q_2 for the first time.

(c) *read rd* is allowed to accesses class 2 quorum Q_2 for the second time: perhaps to "confirm" the value in $Q_1 \cap Q_2$ and to write it for the first time in $Q_2 \setminus Q_1$.

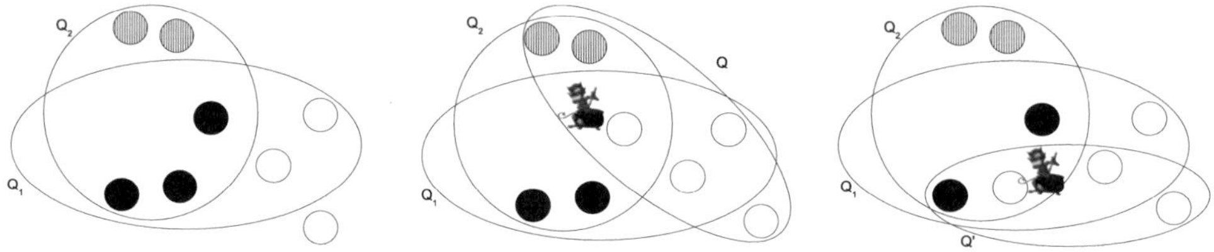

(d) However, if *write* is incomplete, writer might have not yet reached processes from $Q_1 \setminus Q_2$. *read rd* cannot tell the difference...

(e) Yet, this is ok, if Q_2 has a masking quorum intersection with some other quorum Q accessed in the following *read* rd', even if some process is Byzantine. Here, $C_{2a}(Q_2, Q, B)$ holds for any $B \in \boldsymbol{B_1}$.

(f) Masking quorum intersections between Q_2 and some class 3 quorum are not needed if the intersection $Q_1 \cap Q_2$ acts as a dissemination quorum. Indeed, if rd' accesses first Q' for which $C_{2b}(Q_2, Q', B)$ holds for any $B \in \boldsymbol{B_1}$, rd' can still deduce the written value (and even detect the Byzantine behavior) because it was "confirmed" by rd in sufficiently many processes.

Figure 6.2: Class-2 intersection property. We assume threshold adversary $\boldsymbol{B_1}$.

of refined quorum systems with no class 1 quorums is useful for optimal fast protocol implementations. Namely, if we let $\boldsymbol{QC_1} = \emptyset$ a refined quorum system given is any dissemination quorum system $\boldsymbol{DQS}$ for adversary $\boldsymbol{B}$ with $\boldsymbol{QC_2} \subseteq \boldsymbol{DQS}$ such that

$$\forall Q_2 \in \boldsymbol{QC_2}, \forall Q \in \boldsymbol{DQS}, \forall B_1, B_2 : Q_2 \cap Q \not\subseteq B_1 \cup B_2.$$

In other words, $(\emptyset, \boldsymbol{QC_2}, \boldsymbol{DQS})$ is a refined quorum system for $\boldsymbol{B}$. Since there are no class 1 quorums and since atomicity is not required, we can "promote" quorums. Namely, consider the following renaming ("promotion") of quorums: let class 2 quorums be class 1' quorums and class 3 quorums class 2' quorums. Then, using $(\emptyset, \boldsymbol{QC_2}, \boldsymbol{DQS})$, we can design non-atomic storage protocols in the unauthenticated model such that, in the common case, *read* and *write* operations access class 1' quorums only once, and class 2' quorums twice.

As an example of such a fast non-atomic storage protocol, notice that, if $\boldsymbol{QC_2} = \boldsymbol{DQS}$, then $\boldsymbol{DQS}$ is a masking quorum system, and every quorum is a class 1' quorum. This is precisely the quorum system that underlies the single-round MR protocol (Sec. 5.2.2) in which all operations access a quorum only once. An example of a more general protocol with $\boldsymbol{QC_2} \neq \boldsymbol{DQS}$) can be found in [Abraham et al., 2006].

(Uniform) t−refined quorum systems. We define t−refined quorum systems analogously to their counterparts in Chapter 5.

Definition 6.7 **t−refined quorum systems** Given the adversary $\boldsymbol{B_t}$, a refined quorum system is a t-refined quorum system if its resilience is at least t.

Recall that in a uniform refined quorum system, all quorums are class 1 quorums. The following results applicable to uniform t−refined quorum systems can be easily shown using the proofs of the similar results proved in Sec. 5.1.1 in the context of dissemination quorum systems.

Lemma 6.8 *In a uniform t-refined quorum system $\boldsymbol{tMQS}$, all quorums intersect in at least $4t+1$ elements.*

Lemma 6.9 *No uniform t-refined quorum system can be constructed over S if $n = |S| \leq 5t$.*

Theorem 6.10 **Load** $\mathcal{L}(\boldsymbol{utRQS}) \geq \sqrt{\frac{4t+1}{n}}$ for any uniform t-refined quorum system $\boldsymbol{utRQS}$.

Uniform t−refined quorum systems have been widely used in fast protocol implementations. Simple to understand, these are quorum systems designed for the threshold adversary in which all quorums are class 1 quorums, allowing for any common-case operation to complete in a single quorum access. As stipulated by Lemma 6.9, these quorum systems require at least $n = 5t+1$ processes. Assuming $n = 5t+1$, we can construct a uniform t−refined quorum system in which all subsets of size $n - t = 4t + 1$ are class 1 quorums. This is exactly the quorum system used in fast replication protocols that require $5t + 1$ servers [Abd-El-Malek et al., 2005, Martin and Alvisi, 2006]. These protocols were one of the very first to provide a latency-optimized service that tolerates Byzantine faults requiring a quorum to be accessed only once.

Remark 6.11 Uniform $t-$resilient refined quorum systems might be confused with $t-$opaque quorum systems, due to their similar lower bound on the number of processes (see Lemma 6.9 and Theorem 5.29). However, the two families of quorum systems are decisively different.

Optimal resilience. In general, refined quorum systems can be optimally resilient as well, unlike the above mentioned uniform $t-$resilient variant. For example, it is not difficult to see that $(\{S\}, \boldsymbol{Maj}_{\frac{2}{3}}, \boldsymbol{Maj}_{\frac{2}{3}})$ is a $t-$refined quorum system with the set of all nodes S is a class 1 quorum whereas any two-third majority is a class 2 quorum. This quorum system was used in, e.g., Zyzzyva [Kotla et al., 2009] to allow an optimally resilient replication protocol expedite a common-case operation accessing all servers. In refined quorum system terminology, the set of all servers is in this case a class 1 quorum; therefore, it can safely be accessed only once.

Class-2 intersection. Class-2 intersection property is important to allow implementations that achieve both the best possible latency (e.g., 1 round in storage) and the next best possible latency (2 rounds in case of storage). Indeed, consider the following example in which there are 6 servers $S = \{s_1, s_2, s_3, s_4, s_5, s_6\}$, with adversary structure given by

$$\boldsymbol{B} = \{\emptyset, \{s_1\}, \{s_2\}, \{s_3\}, \{s_4\}, \{s_1, s_2\}, \{s_3, s_4\}, \{s_2, s_4\}\}$$

with 3 quorums, $Q_1 = \{s_2, s_4, s_5, s_6\}$, $Q_2 = \{s_1, s_2, s_3, s_4, s_5\}$ and $Q_2' = \{s_1, s_2, s_3, s_4, s_6\}$, it is not difficult to verify that $(\{Q_1\}, \{Q_1, Q_2, Q_2'\}, \{Q_1, Q_2, Q_2'\})$ is a refined quorum system. Indeed, Q_1 is a class 1 quorum, whereas Q_2 and Q_2' are class 2 quorums. This refined quorum system is depicted in Figure 6.3

Figure 6.4(a) depicts several executions of a possible common-case latency efficient atomic SWMR storage algorithm built over this refined quorum system.

In execution ex_1 synchronous $write(1)$ (we denote by wr) accesses a class 1 quorum Q_1 and completes in a single round. In ex_2, wr completes as in ex_1 (although s_1 and s_3 are correct). Therefore, in ex_2, synchronous and uncontended $read$ rd must return value 1 after 2 rounds of communication with servers from Q_2. Moreover, the reader that invokes rd (say r_1) cannot distinguish ex_2 from ex_3 in which wr is slow, concurrent with rd and does not access server s_6. If we extend ex_3 such that s_5 crashes and servers from $B_{12} = \{s_1, s_2\} \in \boldsymbol{B}$ are Byzantine and "forget" about round 2 of rd, we obtain ex_4. In ex_4, $read$ rd' invoked by reader $r_2 \neq r_1$ (upon completion of rd) must eventually return 1; however, at first, it is not clear that rd' should return the value in ex_4 after communicating only with servers from Q_2'. However, rd' in ex_4 is indistinguishable from rd' in ex_5 in which rd is simply slow and in which rd' must return a value while accessing servers from Q_2' since all servers from Q_2' are correct. Hence, in both ex_4 and ex_5, rd' must return 1.

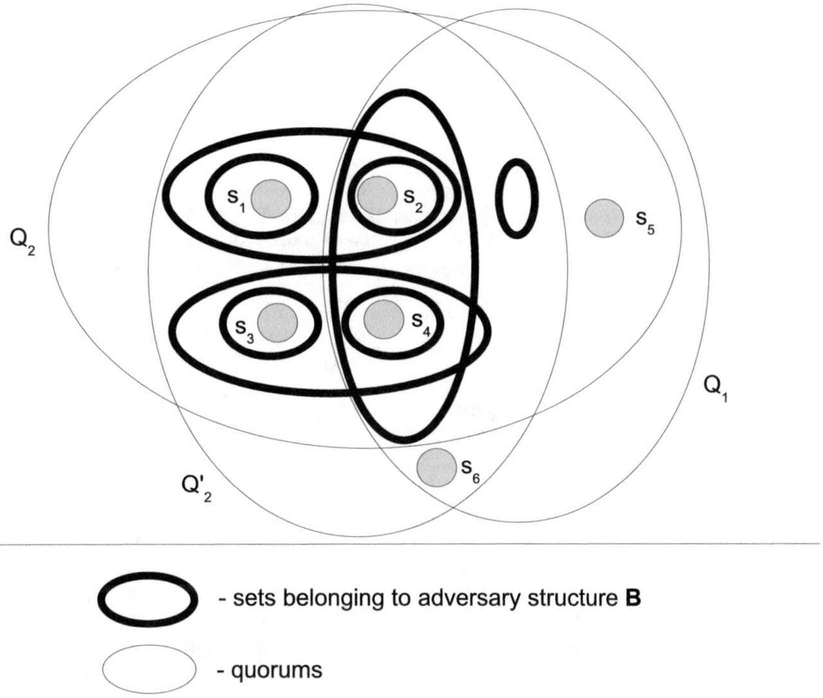

Figure 6.3: Intuition behind Class-2 intersection property: an example of a refined quorum system.

However, notice that, in ex_5, reader r_2 has (just) enough information to return 1, only because Class-2 intersection property holds. For example, since $B_{34} = Q_2 \cap Q'_2 \setminus B_{12} = \{s_3, s_4\} \in \boldsymbol{B}$, $C_{2a}(Q_2, Q'_2, B_{12})$ does not hold and consequently neither does $C_{2a}(Q_2, Q'_2, B_{34})$. Hence, by Lemma 6.5, $C_{2b}(Q_2, Q'_2, B_{34})$ must hold, i.e., $Q_1 \cap Q_2 \cap Q'_2 \not\subseteq B_{34}$. In our case $Q_1 \cap Q_2 \cap Q'_2 \setminus B_{34} = \{s_2\}$, i.e., server s_2 (that was accessed in the first round of wr) is crucial for the ability of reader r_2 to return 1 in rd'.

Indeed, consider the case of a "broken" refined quorum system (identified by subscript $_b$): where $\boldsymbol{RQS_b} = \boldsymbol{QC_{2b}} = \{Q_{1b}, Q_2, Q'_2\}$, with $Q_{1b} = Q_1 \setminus \{s_2\} = \{s_4, s_5, s_6\} \in \boldsymbol{QC_{1b}}$. The refined quorum system $(\boldsymbol{QC_{1b}}, \boldsymbol{QC_{2b}}, \boldsymbol{RQS_b})$ is "broken" in a sense that it violates Class-2 intersection property (but not the Class 1 intersection nor Class-3 intersection). Namely: a) $C_{2a}(Q_2, Q'_2, B_{34})$ does not hold and b) since $Q_{1b} \cap Q_2 \cap Q'_2 \subseteq B_{34}$, $Q_{2b}(Q_2, Q'_2, B_{34})$ does not hold either (unlike in the original, correct refined quorum system described earlier). Executions ex'_1 to ex'_5 depicted in Figure 6.4(b) assume the "broken" refined quorum system $(\boldsymbol{QC_{1b}}, \boldsymbol{QC_{2b}}, \boldsymbol{RQS_b})$ and are, respectively, obtained from executions ex_1 to ex_5 when Q_1 is replaced with Q_{1b} (i.e., when wr does not write in server s_2). Then, we can construct execution ex'_6 similar to ex'_5 (see Fig. 6.4(b)) in which (i) servers

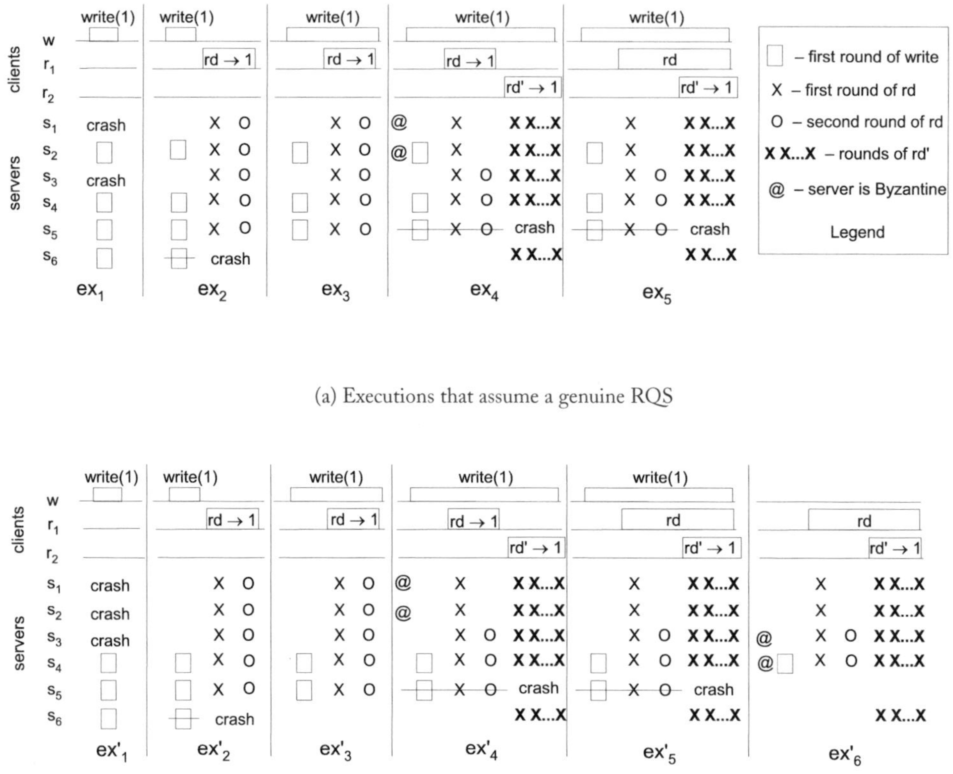

(a) Executions that assume a genuine RQS

(b) Executions that assume a "broken" RQS that violates Class-2 intersection

Figure 6.4: Intuition behind Class-2 intersection property: executions of a possible atomic storage implementation.

from B_{34} are Byzantine, (ii) s_5 is slow and (iii) there is no wr (i.e., value 1 is never written). However, reader r_2 cannot distinguish ex'_6 from ex'_5 and returns 1 in ex'_6, although 1 was never written. This violation of atomicity is a direct consequence of the violation of the Class-2 intersection property.

Finally, notice that the server s_2 in $Q_1 \cap Q_2 \cap Q'_2 \setminus B_{34}$ (in the correct refined quorum system) would not be important if $C_{2a}(Q_2, Q'_2, B_{12})$ held, i.e., if B_{34} would remain outside $\boldsymbol{B}$. Then, in any execution, there would be at least one benign server in B_{34} and the reader would not have to worry about intersections of class 2 quorums with their class 1 counterparts.

6.3 EMULATIONS

In this section we discuss two implementations that rely on refined quorum systems. First (Sec. 6.3.1), we instantiate refined quorum systems in the crash-fault model and describe the FastSynod consensus algorithm of the Fast Paxos replication protocol [Lamport, 2006]. Then, we turn to refined quorum systems in the unauthenticated Byzantine fault model by presenting a SWMR atomic storage implementation, called GV [Guerraoui and Vukolić, 2010].

6.3.1 FAST CONSENSUS

FastSynod is the variant of the Synod consensus protocol we presented in Sec. 4.2. The motivation for FastSynod is drawn from the suboptimal latency of the Synod protocol.

Namely, in the common case, which subsumes a single leader and a synchronous period, Synod requires five message delays for learners to learn a value. Namely, the first message delay is related to a message sent by a proposer to the leader. Then the leader invokes SynodOFC obstruction-free consensus which takes additional four message delays, two in each phase.

It is not difficult to design a variant of Synod in which the two message delays related to the Phase 1 of SynodOFC can be skipped. Indeed, we can designate a dedicated initial leader, which may skip Phase 1 since no value is proposed. This optimization is motivated by practical considerations when Synod is used in context of the Paxos replication protocol which runs several consensus instances in parallel. Then, Phase 1 can be simply executed for all consensus instances simultaneously, thus effectively reducing the latency of the core consensus protocol. The latency of the optimized Synod is then captured by a message from a proposer to leader and two message delays in Phase 2 of SynodOFC.

The question that motivates FastSynod is whether this latency can be further reduced to two message delays? This would clearly be optimal, since in any non-trivial consensus setup that involves at least two proposers and learners, it is straightforward to see that a single message delay latency cannot be achieved even in the common case.

The answer to the above question is affirmative; however, classical quorum systems do not suffice. In order to achieve two message delay consensus latency in the common-case, FastSynod needs a refined quorum system $(\mathcal{QC}_1, \mathcal{QS}, \mathcal{QS})$, for any quorum system $\mathcal{QS}$.

Notation 6.12 Since $(\mathcal{QC}_1, \mathcal{QS}, \mathcal{QS})$ has only two quorum classes, in this section, we refer to class 1 quorums of this quorum system as *fast* quorums and to class 2 quorums as classic quorums.

More specifically, FastSynod achieves two message delay latency (compared to three message delays in optimized Synod), if there are no two concurrent proposals, the system is synchronous and a fast quorum is available. If instead of a fast quorum a classic quorum is available, FastSynod gracefully degrades to achieve three message delay latency. However, if the system is asynchronous or if there are concurrent proposals (we talk about proposal *collisions*), latency of FastSynod can be more than three message delays.

Conceptually, FastSynod is a rather simple variant of the Synod protocol. Namely, upon proposing a value, proposers send a message directly to acceptors (we refer to a *fast proposal*). If acceptors have been initialized to a fast ballot number (as explained in the following), they accept this proposal as if it would be coming in a $p2$ message of the Synod protocol. Learners learn a value with a fast ballot number only if they receive $p2ack$ messages from a fast quorum of acceptors. However, SynodOFC needs to be modified to account for fast proposals — the resulting protocol is called FastSynodOFC.

The wrapper code around FastSynodOFC and Ω is given in Algorithm 25.

Algorithm 25 FastSynod implementation using FastSynodOFC and Ω (proposer p pseudocode)

Local variables initialization: $val \leftarrow any$; $decision \leftarrow abort$

1: **upon** $inv_p(FastSynod, propose(v))$ **do**
2:     $inv_p(FastSynodOFC, fastpropose(v, leader()))$
3:     periodically $send(propose, v)$ to $leader()$
4: **end upon**
5: **upon** $receive\ (propose, v)$ from some proposer **do**
6:     $val \leftarrow v$
7: **end upon**
8: **loop**
9:     **if** $p = leader()$ and $decision = abort$ **then**
10:         $decision \leftarrow inv_p(FastSynodOFC, propose(val))$
11:     **end if**
12: **end loop**

Fast proposal setup. The major change in FastSynod with respect to the Synod protocol is the introduction of the special value any (that is assumed not to be a valid consensus value). Initially, all proposers are initialized with value val equal to any; val changes only upon a proposer invokes $propose(v)$ on FastSynod. However, unlike in classical Synod, the leader does not wait to receive a proposal value from another proposer, but rather directly proposes any to FastSynodOFC (lines 8-12, Algorithm 25). By doing this, leader informs acceptors to allow fast proposals from all proposers.

Namely, when the leader l proposes value any to FastSynodOFC (see Algorithm 26), it executes Phase 1 just like in the classic SynodOFC, with **leaderSelect** procedure slightly modified, as explained later. If no acceptor previously accepted a value (i.e., no value other than any was previously proposed), **leaderSelect** (see Algorithm 29) will retain any as the proposal $value$. Then, the leader marks proposal locally as fast by setting $fastEnabled$ to $true$ (line 19, Algorithm 26) and sends any in a $p2$ message to acceptors, with a ballot number $ballot_p$.

Algorithm 26 FastSynodOFC implementation (pseudocode of proposer p)

Local variables initialization: $ballot_p \leftarrow p - \mathcal{P}$; $val \leftarrow \perp$; $fastEnabled \leftarrow false$

1: **upon** $inv_p(FastSynodOFC, fastpropose(v), p')$ **do**
2:     $send(p2fast, v)$ to all acceptors
3:     $send(propose, v)$ to proposer p'
4: **end upon**

5: **upon** $inv_p(FastSynodOFC, propose(v))$ **do**
6:     **if** $fastEnabled = false$ **then**
7:         $ballot_p \leftarrow ballot_p + \mathcal{P}$
8:         **Phase 1:**
9:             $send(p1, ballot_p)$ to all acceptors
10:             **when** $receive\ (p1ack, ballot_p, bal_i, val_i)$ **or** $(p1abort, ballot_p)$
                from all a_i from some $Q \in \mathbf{QS}$
11:                 **if** received some $p1abort$ **then**
12:                     **return** $abort$
13:                 **end if**
14:                 **leaderSelect**(received $p1ack$ messages, Q, val, v)
15:             **end when**
16:     **end if**
17:     **Phase 2:**
18:         **if** $val = any$ **then**
19:             $fastEnabled \leftarrow true$
20:             **trigger** ⟨ **detectCollisions**$(ballot_p)$ ⟩
21:         **else**
22:             $fastEnabled \leftarrow false$
23:         **end if**
24:         $send(p2, ballot_p, val)$ to all acceptors
25:         **when** $receive\ (p2abort, ballot_p)$
26:             **return** $abort$
27:         **end when**
28: **end upon**

29: **upon** $receive\ (propose, v)$ from proposer p' **do**
30:     $inv_p(FastSynodOFC, propose(v))$
31: **end upon**

On receiving $(p2, ballot, v)$ with $v = any$ from the leader p, an acceptor marks locally the proposal as *fast* (lines 17- 18, Algorithm 27), by setting locally $fastEnabled$ to $true$, $fastBallot$ to $ballot$ and $fastLeader$ to p. Acceptor then does not send $p2ack$ to learners immediately but enables processing of $p2fast$ that carry fast proposals.

Remark 6.13 In FastSynod, fast proposal setup is not counted towards consensus latency. We measure consensus latency from the moment some proposer p receives a $inv_p(FastSynod, propose(v))$ invocation, which is assumed to happen after fast proposal setup is done. When FastSynod is implemented in a full fledged replication protocol, fast proposal setup can be done by the leader for many consensus instances at once.

Processing fast proposals. In the common case, the system is synchronous and the output of Ω is assumed to be stable, i.e., the leader does not change. Under these conditions, FastSynod enables a value to be learned in 2 (resp., 3) message delays if a fast (resp., classic) quorum of acceptors is available and if there are no *collisions*, i.e., if only a single correct proposer *fastproposes* a value.

When proposer p receives a $inv_p(FastSynod, propose(v))$ invocation, p invokes a $fastpropose$ on FastSynodOFC and then periodically sends its proposal value to the leader like in the classic Synod (lines 1-4, Algorithm 25). The $fastpropose$ invocation involves sending $(p2fast, v)$ *directly* to acceptors and forwarding the proposal to the leader using a $propose$ message, similarly as in the classic Synod. We explain both of these message paths that are executed in parallel.

When an acceptor a receives $(p2fast, v)$, if $fastEnabled$ is $true$ locally at a (lines 28- 31, Algorithm 27), a updates its local value to v, sets $p2ballot$ to $fastBallot$ to record that a has casted a vote in $fastBallot$ and sends $(p2fastack, p2ballot, v)$ to all learners and $fastLeader$. Learners use $p2fastack$ messages to learn v in case they receive the same $(p2fastack, ballot, v)$ from a fast quorum of acceptors (line 4, Algorithm 28). On the other hand, the leader of the $fastBallot$ uses $p2fastack$ messages to detect collisions and abort the current instance of FastSynodOFC in case of concurrently proposed values. Collision detection is explained later.

On the other hand, when the leader p_l receives $propose$ message with value v, it invokes $inv_{p_l}(FastSynodOFC, propose(v))$ (lines 29-31, Algorithm 26). Since $fastEnabled$ is $true$ at p_l, l skips the Phase 1 in this proposal (p_l already completed Phase 1, during fast proposal setup) and executes Phase 2 of $fastBallot$ with value v. This guarantees (in absence of collisions) that a correct leader will learn v in three message delays if a fast quorum is unavailable (when two message delays learning might not succeed) but a classic quorum is available.

So far, we described how FastSynod proceeds in the common-case. However, the critical point in FastSynod is when there are two (or more) concurrent fast proposal that may result in collisions. In this case, SynodOFC **leaderSelect** procedure no longer works and needs to be modified. In addition, it is not clear how a leader can detect a collision and abort, since collisions could not occur in the classic Synod. In the following we overview how FastSynodOFC deals with these issues.

Algorithm 27 FastSynodOFC implementation (acceptors pseudocode)

Local variables initialization: $p1ballot \leftarrow 0$; $p2ballot \leftarrow 0$; $val \leftarrow \bot$; $fastEnabled \leftarrow$
 $false$; $fastBallot \leftarrow 0$;
 $fastLeader \leftarrow \bot$

1: **upon** $receive$ $(p1, ballot)$ from some proposer p **do**
2:    **if** $p1ballot \geq ballot$ **or** $p2ballot \geq ballot$ **then**
3:       $send(p1abort, ballot)$ to p
4:    **else**
5:       $p1ballot \leftarrow ballot$
6:       **if** $fastEnabled$ **then**
7:          $send(p2abort, fastBallot)$ to proposer $fastLeader$
8:       **end if**
9:       $fastEnabled \leftarrow false$
10:      $send(p1ack, ballot, p2bal, val)$ to p
11:   **end if**
12: **end upon**

13: **upon** $receive$ $(p2, ballot, v)$ from some proposer p **do**
14:    **if** $p1ballot > ballot$ **or** $p2ballot > ballot$ **then**
15:       $send(p2abort, ballot)$ to p
16:    **else**
17:       **if** $val = any$ **then**   {*Enable acceptance of fast proposals*}
18:          $\langle fastEnabled, fastBallot, fastLeader \rangle \leftarrow \langle true, ballot, p \rangle$
19:          **else if** $p2ballot < ballot$ **or** $(p2ballot = ballot \wedge val = v)$ **then**   {*Acceptor did not cast vote or*
          can repeat the fast vote}
20:             $\langle p2ballot, fastEnabled, val \rangle \leftarrow \langle ballot, false, v \rangle$
21:             $send(p2ack, ballot, v)$ to all learners
22:             **if** $ballot = fastBallot$ **then**
23:                $send(p2ack, ballot, v)$ to proposer p
24:             **end if**
25:       **end if**
26:    **end if**
27: **end upon**

28: **upon** $receive$ $(p2fast, v)$ from some proposer p **and** $fastEnabled$ **do**
29:    $\langle fastEnabled, p2ballot, val \rangle \leftarrow \langle false, fastBallot, v \rangle$
30:    $send(p2fastack, p2ballot, v)$ to all learners and $fastLeader$
31: **end upon**

Algorithm 28 FastSynodOFC implementation (learners pseudocode)

upon $receive$ $(p2ack, ballot, v)$ from all a_i from some $Q \in \boldsymbol{QS}$ **do**
    return $learn(v)$
end upon
upon $receive$ $(p2fastack, ballot, v)$ from all a_i from some fast quorum $Q_1 \in \boldsymbol{QC_1}$ **do**
    return $learn(v)$
end upon

Preserving consistency. Before discussing consistency, we first define the notion of a *fast chosen* value.

Definition 6.14 Fast chosen If a fast quorum of acceptors accepts v by receiving $(p2fast, v)$ messages in $fastBallot$, we say that v is *fast chosen* in $fastBallot$.

In FastSynodOFC, just like in SynodOFC, the **leaderSelect** procedure is critical for maintaining consensus safety across different ballot numbers. However, in FastSynodOFC, having a leader choose the value with maximum ballot number among received $p1ack$ messages no longer works because multiple proposals can exist in the same ballot.

Indeed, to see why, assume that there are two fast proposals with values $v \neq v'$ in $fastBallot$. Assume also that some learner learns v. Hence, there is a fast quorum Q_1 of acceptors that accepted v (i.e., v is fast chosen in $fastBallot$), but some acceptor $a \notin Q_1$ might have accepted v' in $fastBallot$, then, when the leader changes, reusing the **leaderSelect** procedure from SynodOFC might result in picking v' for next ballot, thus violating consensus Agreement.

To cope with this, FastSynodOFC needs to modify the **leaderSelect** procedure to account for possibility of fast proposal learning and collisions (Algorithm 29). To this end, **leaderSelect** retrieves a *set* V of all, possibly different, values with the highest ballot number in received $p1ack$ messages (line 3, Algorithm 29). If V contains at most one value, the value val is selected as in SynodOFC. However, if V contains at least two values, val is selected as follows (line 4, Algorithm 29): denoting the quorum of acceptors from which the leader received $p1ack$ messages by Q, if there is a fast quorum Q_1 such that all acceptors from $Q_1 \cap Q$ replied with value $v' \in V$, then v' is selected as val. It is very important to notice that the Class-1 intersection property of refined quorum systems guarantees uniqueness of such a value v', indeed if the above predicate would hold for some other value $v'' \neq v'$ and fast quorum $Q_2 \neq Q_1$, since Class-1 intersection property mandates $Q_1 \cap Q_2 \cap Q \neq \emptyset$, this would imply that one acceptor accepted two different values in $fastBallot$ which is impossible. This guarantees that the following Lemma holds.

Lemma 6.15 *If a value v is chosen (Def. 4.5) or fast chosen in b, then an acceptor can only accept v in ballots higher than b.*

Algorithm 29 FastSynodOFC implementation (proposers' subroutines)

1: **procedure leaderSelect**($msgs$, Q, val, v)
2:     $maxbal \leftarrow$ maximum $m.bal_i$ for $m \in msgs$
3:     $V \leftarrow \{v'\} : \exists m \in msgs$ with $m.bal_i = maxbal$ and $m.val_i = v'$
4:     **if** $|V| > 1$ **and** $\exists v' \in V, \exists Q_1 \in QC_1, \forall m \in msgs, \forall a_i \in Q_1 \cap Q : m.val_i = v'$ **then**
5:         $val \leftarrow v'$
6:     **else if** $\exists maxv \in V : maxv \neq \perp$ **then**
7:         $val \leftarrow maxv$
8:     **else**
9:         $val \leftarrow v$
10:     **end if**
11: **end procedure**

Module: detectCollisions($ballot$)
Local variables initialization: $ballotValues \leftarrow \{\}$
12: **upon** $receive\ (p2ack, ballot, v)$ **or** $(fastp2ack, ballot, v)$ **do**
13:     $ballotValues \leftarrow ballotValues \cup \{v\}$
14: **end upon**
15: **upon** $|ballotValues| > 1$ **do**
16:     **return** $abort$
17: **end upon**

Detecting collisions. After the leader completes the fast proposal setup by sending *any* value in $p2$ to acceptors, it needs to ensure that a value will be eventually learned by learners, or that it aborts the *propose* invocation in order to ensure OF Termination (see Sec. 4.2).[2] OFC abort in case of a collision is critical since it allows the leader to restart the loop in lines 8-12 (Algorithm 25) and guarantee consensus Termination.

To this end, in a *fastBallot*, acceptors simply inform *fastLeader* of any vote they send to learners. This is captured in lines 22-24 and 30 in acceptors' code (Algorithm 27). The **collisionDetection** module at leaders (Algorithm 29) simply collects all the *p2ack* and *p2fastack* messages received from acceptors and returns *abort* in case it detects two different values in *fastBallot*.

Threshold-based quorum systems. We emphasize two special cases of the (QC_1, QS, QS) refined quorum system that underlies FastSynod. These special, threshold based cases, are the ones most often used in the variants of the FastSynod protocol [Lamport, 2006, Zielinski, 2006].

---

[2]Strictly speaking, if no proposer fast proposes a value, OF Termination might be violated when the leader proposes *any*. Therefore, we assume that OF Termination must apply to *propose* invocation that proposes the special value *any* only if it is followed by a fast proposal by some proposer.

- If $\boldsymbol{QC_1} = \boldsymbol{QS}$ and assuming that a quorum system $\boldsymbol{QS}$ needs to be $t-$resilient, an example of a quorum system that might be used in FastSynod is the two thirds majority quorum system $\boldsymbol{Maj_{\frac{2}{3}}}$ with $n = 3t + 1$ and every subset containing $2t + 1$ acceptors being a fast quorum. This quorum system has only fast quorums.

- If FastSynod needs to be optimally resilient, than for classic quorums in FastSynod classical majorities can be used (with $n = 2t + 1$, any set containing at least $t + 1$ acceptors is a quorum). Then, let every quorum containing $n - f$ acceptors be fast quorum. Then, Class-1 intersection property mandates that $n \geq t + 2f + 1$, suggesting $f = \lfloor \frac{n}{4} \rfloor$ as a possible solution for the size of fast quorums. For example, with $n = 5$ acceptors, every set of $n - f = 4$ (or more) acceptors can be a fast quorum and every set of 3 acceptors can be a classic quorum.

6.3.2 FAST BYZANTINE STORAGE

With FastSynod, we exemplified the power of refined quorum systems in the crash-case. We now turn to demonstrating the full-fledged refined quorum system based emulation, called GV [Guerraoui and Vukolić, 2010], that implements SWMR wait-free atomic storage in the asynchronous unauthenticated Byzantine fault model. In general, wait-free storage emulations in unauthenticated model, especially those with atomic semantics are rather involved, regardless of the latency requirements.

Given adversary $\boldsymbol{B}$, GV assumes a refined quorum system $\boldsymbol{RQS} = (\boldsymbol{QC_1}, \boldsymbol{QC_2}, \boldsymbol{QC_3})$ over a set of server processes S, guarantees atomicity and wait-freedom. Moreover, GV optimizes common-case latency, ensuring the following desirable property: all synchronous and uncontended $read/write$ operations complete in:

1. 1 communication round (2 message delays) if a class 1 quorum is available (i.e., if $\exists Q_1 \in \boldsymbol{QC_1} : Q_1 \subseteq alive(S)$);

2. 2 communication rounds (4 message delays) if a class 2 quorum is available (i.e., if $\exists Q_2 \in \boldsymbol{QC_2} : Q_2 \subseteq alive(S)$); and

3. 3 communication rounds (6 message delays) if a class 3 quorum is available (i.e., if $\exists Q_3 \in \boldsymbol{QC_3} : Q_3 \subseteq alive(S)$).

Besides, GV tolerates crash faults of all clients, both readers and the writer. In the following, if an operation op completes in i communication rounds (or, simply, rounds), we talk about a $i-$round op.

6.3.2.1 Overview.

The pseudocode of GV is given in Algorithms 30 ($write$ pseudocode at client), 31 (server pseudocode) and 32 and 33 ($read$ pseudocode).

Pseudocode of a $write$ (Algorithm 30) is relatively simple and consists of at most three rounds of interactions between the client (writer) and servers. If $write$ is synchronous and a class i quorum is available, $write$ completes in i rounds ($i \in \{1, 2, 3\}$). Notably, the writer keeps track of class 2 quorums that respond in the first round, in order to ensure that the writer communicated with the same class 2 quorum in both rounds in the case of a 2-round write.

On the other hand, $read$ is more involved. Nevertheless, $read$ implementation in GV resembles that of ABD. Namely, $read$ is split in two phases:

1. the Read phase that implements *regular* storage (lines 4-19, Algorithm 32); and

2. the Writeback phase that enforces atomicity, in which the readers write value back to a "sufficient" number of servers (Algorithm 34).

The key feature of the GV Read phase is that it always completes in a single round, so long as $read$ is synchronous and uncontended. Then, in the Writeback phase, the reader evaluates refined quorum intersections and the responses from servers received in the Read phase and: 1) does not perform any actual writeback in case a class 1 quorum was accessed in the Read phase; and 2) performs additionally 1 (resp., 2) rounds of writeback in case a class 2 (resp., 3) quorum is available.

In the following, we first explain the details behind GV $write$ and then turn to $read$.

6.3.2.2 Write operation.

A $write$ operation consists of at most three rounds (see Algorithm 30). In each round $i \in \{1, 2, 3\}$ (lines 16-28, Algorithm 30), the writer sends a $(write, ts, v, \boldsymbol{accessedQC_2}, i)$ (line 18, Algorithm 30) message containing timestamp ts and value v, as well as a subset of class 2 quorums $\boldsymbol{accessedQC_2}$ (this set is used only in round 2, being empty in rounds 1 and 3). In every round, the writer awaits acks from some quorum and, in the first two rounds, the expiration of the timer set to 2Δ (line 25, Algorithm 30). GV $write$ distinguishes three cases:

1. If the writer accesses some class 1 quorum in the first round, the write completes (line 4, Algorithm 30) in a single round.

2. Else, if in round 1, the writer accessed some class 2 quorums, these quorums are stored into local variable $\boldsymbol{accessedQC_2}$ (line 7, Algorithm 30). If in round 2, the writer accesses once again some quorum from $\boldsymbol{accessedQC_2}$, $write$ completes at the end of round 2.

3. Else, the writer proceeds to round 3 and completes at the end of this round, upon accessing any quorum in round 3.

Upon reception of $(write, ts, v, \boldsymbol{accessedQC_2}, i)$ message (lines 1-9, Algorithm 31), a server s_j stores the received data locally in its $history_j$ matrix — rows of $history_j$ are indexed by timestamps whereas there are 3 $history_j$ columns. More specifically, upon receiving a $write$ message sent in round i of a $write$, s_j stores $history_j[ts, k].pair = \langle ts, v \rangle$ for all k such that $1 \leq k \leq i$ and adds $\boldsymbol{accessedQC_2}$ to $history_j[ts, i].sets$ (see Algorithm 31). Notice that a server never overwrites

---

Algorithm 30 GV storage algorithm: *write* code at the client

---

Local variables initialization: $ts \leftarrow 0$; $timeout \leftarrow 2\Delta$; $accessed\,QC_2 \leftarrow \emptyset$; $accessed \leftarrow \emptyset$

1: **upon** $inv_c(GV, write(v))$ **do**
2:   $ts \leftarrow ts + 1$
3:   $accessed \leftarrow$ **round**(1)
4:   **if** $\exists Q_1 \in QC_1 : Q \subseteq accessed$ **then**   *{Class 1 quorum was accessed}*
5:     **return** $resp_c(GV, ack)$
6:   **end if**
7:   $accessed\,QC_2 \leftarrow \{Q_2 \in QC_2 : Q_2 \subseteq accessed\}$
8:   $accessed \leftarrow$ **round**(2)
9:   **if** $\exists Q_2 \in accessed\,QC_2 : Q_2 \subseteq accessed$ **then**   *{Same Class 2 quorum was again accessed}*
10:     **return** $resp_c(GV, ack)$
11:   **end if**
12:   $accessed\,QC_2 \leftarrow \emptyset$;
13:   $accessed \leftarrow$ **round**(3)
14:   **return** $resp_c(GV, ack)$
15: **end upon**

16: **function round**(i)
17:   $accessed \leftarrow \emptyset$
18:   *send* $(write, ts, v, accessed\,QC_2, i)$ to all servers
19:   **if** $i = 1$ **or** $i = 2$ **then**
20:     **trigger**($timeout$)
21:   **end if**
22:   **upon** $receive$ $(writeAck, ts, i)$ from server s_j **do**
23:     $accessed \leftarrow resp \cup \{s_j\}$
24:   **end upon**
25:   **upon** $\exists Q \in RQS : Q \subseteq accessed$ **and** $timeout$ expires **do**
26:     **return** $accessed$
27:   **end upon**
28: **end function**

$history_j[*.*].pair$ data (line 3, Algorithm 31). Then, a server replies to the client via a $writeAck$ message (line 8, Algorithm 31).

Algorithm 31 GV storage algorithm: server s_j code

Local variables initialization: $history_j[*, *].pair \leftarrow \langle 0, \perp \rangle$; $history_j[*, *].sets \leftarrow \emptyset$

1: **upon** $receive$ $(write, ts, v, \boldsymbol{accessed\,QC_2}, i)$ from client c **do**
2:   **for** $k = 1$ to i **do**
3:     **if** $history_j[ts, k], pair = \langle 0, \perp \rangle$ **then**
4:       $history_j[ts, k].pair \leftarrow \langle ts, v \rangle$
5:     **end if**
6:   **end for**
7:   $history_j[ts, i].sets = history_j[ts, i].sets \cup \boldsymbol{accessed\,QC_2}$
8:   $send$ $(writeAck, ts, i)$ to c
9: **end upon**
10: **upon** $receive$ $(read, tsr, i)$ from client c **do**
11:   $send$ $(readAck, tsr, i, history_j)$ to c
12: **end upon**

6.3.2.3 Read operation.

Read phase. The Read phase of $read$ is given in Algorithm 32. The goal of the Read phase is to *select* the timestamp-value pair (line 19, Algorithm 32), with a value that the reader is going to return after a possible writeback. Read phase consists of one or more rounds (lines 5-18, Algorithm 32) in which the reader sends $(read, readCnt, readRnd)$ to all servers (line 10), where $readCnt$ and $readRnd$ serve to distinguish messages sent by the same reader in different operations and, respectively, rounds. A server responds to a $read$ message by sending the entire history of the shared variable in a $readAck$ message (lines 10-12, Algorithm 31). The reader maintains a three-dimensional view of the system history in its $history$ variable, where $history[j]$ serves for storing the latest information about $history_j$ received from server s_j (line 22-25, Algorithm 32). Several predicates are defined in GV to help evaluate the status of the history at the reader as well as quorum intersections to help return the consistent value. These predicates are given in Algorithm 33. We explain their use throughout the algorithm presentation.

A round in the Read phase ends when the reader receives responses from all servers from some quorum Q (line 11, Algorithm 32). The first round is a special one; namely, in round 1, the reader:

- triggers a $timeout$ set to 2Δ (corresponding to 2 message delays, line 7, Algorithm 32) and waits for its expiration to complete round 1 (line 11, Algorithm 32),

- stores all accessed class 2 quorums in local variable $\boldsymbol{accessedQC_2}$ (line 13, Algorithm 32). This will later reveal crucial for allowing 2-round common-case reads and single round common-case writes in the same implementation;
- determines the cutoff timestamp $cutoffTS$ (line 14, Algorithm 32), which is the highest timestamp read by the reader in round 1 of the Read phase, be it from benign or Byzantine servers. Timestamp $cutoffTS$ helps ensure wait freedom.

At the heart of the Read phase are predicates in lines 1-7 of Algorithm 33. Notably, predicates $valid_k$ (for $k \in \{1, 2, 3\}$) (lines 1-3, Algorithm 33) help ensure atomicity. Namely, if a complete $write$ (resp., $read$) operation op wrote (resp., selected) a pair $\langle ts, v\rangle$, in any $read$ rd that follows op, for every quorum Q accessed by the reader in rd there will exist some k such that $valid_k(ts, v, Q)$ holds. Therefore, predicate $invalid(ts, v)$ (line 4, Algorithm 33) cannot hold in rd. This is important for it prevents a reader from selecting an older value than the one written/returned by op (i.e., a pair $\langle ts_{sel}, v_{sel}\rangle$ such that $ts_{sel} < ts$).

To see why this is true, notice that a reader selects $\langle ts_{sel}, v_{sel}\rangle$ in line 19 (Algorithm 33) as the pair with the highest timestamp among all $\langle ts, v\rangle$ pairs for which predicates $highCand(ts, v)$ (line 7, Algorithm 33) and $safe(ts, v)$ hold (line 6, Algorithm 33). Predicate $highCand$ ensures that all pairs with a higher timestamp are $invalid$, i.e., that there are no possibly newer values that ought to be considered for selection.

On the other hand, predicate $safe(ts, v)$ is a necessary check in the unauthenticated model that prevents selection of a timestamp-value pair forged by Byzantine servers. Intuitively, all servers from some set $T \notin \boldsymbol{B}$ need to confirm the pair before a reader can select it. This prevents forging given that, in every execution, T contains at least one benign server.

The following lemma is crucial for the common-case efficiency of GV $read$.

Lemma 6.16 *If $read$ operation rd is synchronous and uncontended, Read phase completes in a single round (2 message delays)*

Proof. *(Sketch.)* Since rd is uncontended, let wr writing the timestamp-value pair $\langle ts, v\rangle$ be the last (complete) write that precedes rd.[3] Regardless of whether wr completed in 1, 2, or 3 rounds, wr wrote $\langle ts, v\rangle$ into some quorum of servers $Q \in \{RQS\}$.

Moreover, it is not difficult to see that no benign server $s_j \in S$ stores any value with a higher timestamp than ts. Since rd is synchronous, and by assumption that $\exists Q_c \in \{RQS\} : Q_c \subseteq alive(S)$, reader will access Q_c in the first round of the Read phase in rd. Since refined quorum systems are a special case of dissemination quorum systems, by Byzantine intersection property we have $Q_c \cap Q = T_c \notin \boldsymbol{B}$. Hence, $safe(ts, v)$ holds at the end of round 1 of Read phase in rd.

Furthermore, is not difficult to see that for any value v' with timestamp $ts' > ts$, none of the predicates $valid_1(ts', v', Q_c)$, $valid_2(ts', v', Q_c)$ and $valid_3(ts', v', Q_c)$ holds. Hence, for any

[3] The proof is similar if no $write$ precedes rd.

Algorithm 32 GV storage algorithm: Read phase of *read*.

1: **upon** $inv_c(GV, read())$ **do**
2:     $readCnt \leftarrow readCnt + 1; readRnd \leftarrow 0;$
3:     $\boldsymbol{accessedQC_2} \leftarrow \emptyset; \boldsymbol{accessedQuorums} \leftarrow \emptyset; accessed \leftarrow \emptyset$
4:     **Phase 1:**   *{Read phase}*
5:       **repeat**
6:         $readRnd \leftarrow readRnd + 1$
7:         **if** $readRnd = 1$ **then**
8:           **trigger**($timeout$)
9:         **end if**
10:        $send\ (read, readCnt, readRnd)$ to all servers
11:        **when** $receive\ (read, readCnt, readRnd, *)$ from some $Q \in \boldsymbol{RQS}$ **and** $timeout$ expires
12:          **if** $readRnd = 1$ **then**
13:            $\boldsymbol{accessedQC_2} \leftarrow \boldsymbol{accessedQuorums} \cap \boldsymbol{QC_2}$
14:            $cutoffTS \leftarrow$ highest $ts \in \mathbb{N}_0 : \exists v \in \mathbb{D}_\perp, \exists s_j \in S : read(ts, v, j)$
15:          **end if**
16:        **end when**
17:        $CandPairs \leftarrow \{\langle ts, v\rangle \in \mathbb{N}_0 \times \mathbb{D}_\perp | safe(ts, v) \wedge highCand(ts, v))\}$
18:      **until** $CandPairs \neq \emptyset$
19:      $\langle ts_{sel}, v_{sel}\rangle \leftarrow \langle ts, v\rangle \in CandPairs$ with highest ts
20:    execute Writeback phase
21: **end upon**

22: **upon** $receive\ (readAck, readCnt, rnd, history_j)$ from server s_j **do**
23:    **if** $rnd = readRnd$ **then**
24:      $history[j] \leftarrow history_j$
25:    **end if**
26:    $accessed \leftarrow accessed \cup \{s_j\}$
27:    $\boldsymbol{accessedQuorums} \leftarrow \{Q \in \boldsymbol{RQS} | Q \subseteq accessed\}$
28: **end upon**

Algorithm 33 GV storage algorithm: reader pseudocode. Initialization and predicates.

Local variables initialization:

$\boldsymbol{accessed\,QC_2} \leftarrow \emptyset$; $\boldsymbol{accessed\,Quorums} \leftarrow \emptyset$; $history[*,*,*] \leftarrow \langle\langle 0, \perp\rangle, \emptyset\rangle$;
$cutoffTS \leftarrow 0$; $readCnt \leftarrow 0$ $readRnd \leftarrow 0$; $timeout \leftarrow 2\Delta$; $accessed \leftarrow \emptyset$; $rec \leftarrow \emptyset$

Predicates and Definitions:

Read phase predicates

$valid_1(ts, v, Q) ::= \exists T \subseteq Q, \forall s_j \in T : (T \notin \boldsymbol{B} \wedge (history[j, ts, 1].pair = \langle ts, v\rangle))$

$valid_2(ts, v, Q) ::= \exists s_j \in Q : history[j, ts, 2].pair = \langle ts, v\rangle$

$valid_3(ts, v, Q) ::= \exists Q_2 \in \boldsymbol{QC_2}, \exists B \in \boldsymbol{B}, \forall s_j \in Q_2 \cap Q \setminus B, \exists \boldsymbol{setsys_j} \subseteq \boldsymbol{QC_2}$:
$(C_{2b}(Q_2, Q, B)) \wedge (history[j, c.ts, 1] = \langle c, \boldsymbol{setsys_j}\rangle) \wedge (Q_2 \in \boldsymbol{setsys_j})$

$invalid(ts, v) ::= \exists Q \in \boldsymbol{accessed\,Quorums}$:
$\neg(valid_1(ts, v, Q) \vee valid_2(ts, v, Q) \vee valid_3(ts, v, Q)) \vee (ts > cutoffTS)$

$read(ts, v, j) ::= \exists rnd \in \{1, 2, 3\} : history[j, ts, rnd].pair = \langle ts, v\rangle$

$safe(ts, v) ::= \{s_j \in S | read(ts, v, j)\} \notin \boldsymbol{B}$

$highCand(ts, v) ::= \forall\langle ts', v'\rangle \in \mathbb{N}_0 \times \mathbb{D}_\perp, \forall s_j \in S$:
$read(ts', v', j) \wedge (ts' > ts) \Rightarrow invalid(ts', v')$

Writeback phase predicates and definitions

$RQSfilter_1(ts, v, R) ::= \exists Q_1 \in \boldsymbol{QC_1}, \exists Q_R \in \boldsymbol{QC_R}, \exists \boldsymbol{setsys} \subseteq \boldsymbol{QC_2} \cup \{\emptyset\}$:
$\bigwedge(Q_1 \cap Q_R \subseteq \{s_j \in S | history[j, ts, R] = \langle\langle ts, v\rangle, \boldsymbol{setsys}\rangle\})$
$\bigwedge(R \neq 2 \vee Q_R \in \boldsymbol{setsys})$

$\boldsymbol{RQSfilter_2}(ts, v, R) ::= \{Q_2 \in \boldsymbol{accessed\,QC_2} | \exists Q_R \in \boldsymbol{QC_R}$:
$Q_R \cap Q_2 \subseteq \{s_j \in S | history[j, ts, R].pair = \langle ts, v\rangle\}\}$

---

such timestamp-value pair $invalid(ts', v')$ holds. Hence, at the end of round 1 of the Read phase in rd, $highCand(ts, v)$ also holds and $CandPairs$ is not empty in line 17, Algorithm 32.

Remark 6.17 Besides, no value with a timestamp smaller than ts can be in $CandPairs$ at the end of round 1. Namely, for any quorum Q that is in $\boldsymbol{accessed\,Quorums}$ at the end of round 1 of rd, there is some j such that $valid_j(ts, v, Q)$ holds. To see this, assume that wr completed either in: (a) single round by accessing class 1 quorum Q_1, or (b) in more than one round. Then, it is not difficult to see that for every quorum Q, in case (a) $valid_1(ts, v, Q)$ holds (by Class-1 intersection property), whereas in case (b) $valid_2(ts, v, Q)$ holds (by Byzantine intersection property). Hence, $invalid(ts, v)$ cannot hold at the end of round 1, i.e., $CandPairs$ is a singleton at the end of round 1 in case of an uncontended and synchronous $read$. □

Finally, notice that the set $CandPairs$ is not necessarily a singleton in case of a contended $read$. Namely, in such a $read$ $CandPairs$ might be empty, or even contain more than a single value (intuitively, the Read phase provides regular semantics only, where multiple values can be returned).

Writeback phase. We now turn to description of the second phase of $read$, the Writeback phase which turns the regular implementation (Read phase) into an atomic one. The code of the Writeback phase is given in Algorithm 34, with auxiliary predicate $RQSfilter_1$ (line 8, Algorithm 33) and set of class 2 quorums $\boldsymbol{RQSfilter_2}$ (line 9, Algorithm 33). These RQS filters dictate the outcome of a Writeback phase, which may take anywhere between 0 and 2 communication rounds. In short, in case of a synchronous and uncontended $read$ that accessed a class 1 quorum in the Read phase, no message is sent in the Writeback phase. Otherwise, if class 2 (resp., class 3) quorum is available, Writeback takes 1 (resp., 2) communication rounds. Hence, when the $read$ is synchronous and uncontended, it completes in at most 3 rounds.

In the Writeback phase, the reader applies RQS filters on the timestamp-value pair $\langle ts_{sel}, v_{sel} \rangle$ selected at the end of Read phase. The outcome governs how many additional writeback rounds would be executed by the reader. Careful writeback to optimize efficiency is targeted in GV only when an operation is synchronous and unconteded. Hence, if $readRnd > 1$ at the beginning of the Writeback phase (line 2, Algorithm 34), indicating that a $read$ is not the common case one, 2 writeback rounds are executed (lines 18 and 19, Algorithm 34). Else if a $read$ is synchronous and uncontended (when $readRnd = 1$ by Lemma 6.16), we distinguish the following cases, assuming that the last complete $write$ that precedes the $read$ completed in R rounds.

1. If the reader accessed a class 1 quorum Q_1 in the Read phase (such that Q_1 contains only benign servers) in round 1, $RQSfilter_1(ts_{sel}, v_{sel}, R)$ holds (line 3, Algorithm 34) and rd completes at the end of round 1, *without* any writeback whatsoever. To see why $RQSfilter_1(ts_{sel}, v_{sel}, R)$ holds in this case, notice that, by line 8, Algorithm 33, $RQSfilter_1(ts_{sel}, v_{sel}, R)$ holds if there is a class 1 quorum Q_1 and a class R quorum Q_R such that *all* servers from $Q_1 \cap Q_R$ had: (a) received a round R $write$ message containing ts and v and (b) later were accessed by the reader. This is precisely the case in our uncontended and synchronous $read$ which is preceded by a R-round $write$.

2. Otherwise, if the reader accessed a class 2 quorum Q_2 in the Read phase (such that Q_2 contains only benign servers) then set $\boldsymbol{RQSfilter_2}(ts_{sel}, v_{sel}, R)$ (defined in line 9, Algorithm 33) is non-empty set of class 2 quorums (since $Q_2 \in \boldsymbol{RQSfilter_2}(ts_{sel}, v_{sel}, R)$). Indeed, notice that $\boldsymbol{RQSfilter_2}(ts_{sel}, v_{sel}, R)$ contains a set of all class 2 quorums Q_2 such that: (a) the reader accessed Q_2 in round 1 of the Read phase of rd (i.e., $Q_2 \in \boldsymbol{accessedQC_2}$), and (b) there is a class R quorum Q_R such that *all* servers from $Q_2 \cap Q_R$ received the round R $write$ message containing ts and v.

When $\boldsymbol{RQSfilter_2}(ts_{sel}, v_{sel}, R)$ is non-empty, we distinguish two cases. First, if $R \in \{2, 3\}$ (line 5, Algorithm 34), then the reader executes **writeback-2** round in which a

---

Algorithm 34 GV storage algorithm: Writeback phase.

1: **Phase 2:**   *{Writeback phase}*
2:   **if** $readRnd = 1$ **then**   *{True if read is synchronous and uncontended}*
3:     **if** $\exists R \in \{1, 2, 3\} : RQSfilter_1(ts_{sel}, v_{sel}, R)$ **then**   *{Class 1 quorum was accessed}*
4:       **return** $resp_c(GV, v_{sel})$
5:     **else if** $\exists R \in \{2, 3\} : RQSfilter_2(ts_{sel}, v_{sel}, R) \neq \emptyset$ **then**
6:       $rec \leftarrow$ **writeback-2**$(ts_{sel}, v_{sel}, \emptyset, false)$
7:       **return** $resp_c(GV, v_{sel})$
8:     **else if** $RQSfilter_2(ts_{sel}, v_{sel}, 1) \neq \emptyset$ **then**
9:       $rec \leftarrow$ **writeback-1**$(ts_{sel}, v_{sel}, RQSfilter_2(ts_{sel}, v_{sel}, 1), true)$
10:       **if** $\exists Q \in RQSfilter_2(ts_{sel}, v_{sel}, 1) : Q \subseteq rec$ **then**
11:         **return** $resp_c(GV, v_{sel})$
12:       **else**
13:         $rec \leftarrow$ **writeback-2**$(ts_{sel}, v_{sel}, \emptyset, false)$
14:         **return** $resp_c(GV, v_{sel})$
15:       **end if**
16:     **end if**
17:   **end if**
18:   $rec \leftarrow$ **writeback-1**$(ts_{sel}, v_{sel}, \emptyset, false)$
19:   $rec \leftarrow$ **writeback-2**$(ts_{sel}, v_{sel}, \emptyset, false)$
20:   **return** $resp_c(GV, v_{sel})$

21: **function writeback-rnd**$(ts, v, setsys, withTimeout)$, with $rnd \in \{1, 2\}$
22:   $rec \leftarrow \emptyset$
23:   **if** $withTimeout$ **then**
24:     **trigger**$(timeout)$
25:   **end if**
26:   $send\ (write, ts, v, setsys, rnd)$ to all servers
27:   **when** $receive\ (writeAck, ts, rnd)$ from server s_j
28:     $rec \leftarrow rec \cup \{s_j\}$
29:   **end when**
30:   **when** $\exists Q \in RQS : Q \subseteq rec$ **and** $timeout$ expires
31:     **return** rec
32:   **end when**
33: **end function**

$(write, ts_{sel}, v_{sel}, \emptyset, 2)$ message is sent to servers, resembling the *write* message sent by the writer in the second round of a *write*. In this case, reader writesback with $rnd = 2$ since it knows that the writer already completed writing the value to some quorum. Namely, writing the value to servers using $(write, ts_{sel}, v_{sel}, \emptyset, rnd)$ message with $rnd = 2$ conveys that the client knows that all servers from some quorum have already stored pair $\langle ts, v\rangle$.

Otherwise, if $R = 1$, the first round of the writeback procedure is more sophisticated, since the reader cannot be sure that all servers from some quorum already stored $\langle ts, v\rangle$ (recall here the executions depicted in Fig. 6.4). Namely, in this case (line 8, Algorithm 34), the reader executes **writeback-1** round with a timeout, which involves (lines 9 and 21-33, Algorithm 34): (a) triggering a timer, (b) sending $(writets_{sel}, v_{sel}, \boldsymbol{RQSfilter_2}(ts_{sel}, v_{sel}, 1), 1)$ to all servers, and (c) waiting for acks from a quorum and expiration of a timer. The uncontended and synchronous *read* completes at the end of round 2 only if the reader accesses again some quorum from $\boldsymbol{RQSfilter_2}(ts_{sel}, v_{sel}, 1)$ in this writeback round (line 10, Algorithm 34).

Writing class 2 quorum IDs contained in the $\boldsymbol{RQSfilter_2}(ts_{sel}, v_{sel}, 1)$, is crucial for allowing 2 round common case reads to be combined with single round common-case writes. For example, if ex_5 of Figure 6.4 is applied to GV, the reader in r_1 would be writing back the value in the second round of *rd* precisely as described above.

3. Otherwise, if no quorum from $\boldsymbol{RQSfilter_2}(ts_{sel}, v_{sel}, 1)$ replies, the second round of the writeback procedure is invoked (line 14, Algorithm 34).

6.4 BIBLIOGRAPHIC NOTES

- Refined quorum systems were introduced in [Guerraoui and Vukolić, 2010]. These quorum systems can be used to reason about many latency-efficient storage, consensus and state-machine replication protocols that implicitly rely on refined quorum systems, such as [Brasileiro et al., 2001, Kotla et al., 2009, Lamport, 2006, Martin and Alvisi, 2006, Zielinski, 2006]. [Guerraoui and Vukolić, 2010] also features optimality proofs of refined quorum systems in the context of atomic storage and consensus, which show that refined quorum system intersection properties are also necessary for common-case latency-efficient implementations.

- Lower bounds for latency-efficient consensus emulations were introduced in [Lamport, 2003]. Refined quorum systems properties generalize these lower bounds stipulated assuming threshold based adversary and threshold-sized quorums.

- Single-round atomic storage emulations in which all *read* and *write* operations complete in a single round, even in the worst case, were considered in [Dutta et al., 2010]. This implementation uses different quorum intersections than those of refined quorums. [Dutta et al.,

2010] also shows that in order to obtain single-round atomic storage emulations, the number of reader processes must be limited.

- The constraint on the limited number of readers of [Dutta et al., 2010] was relaxed in [Georgiou et al., 2009] where "semifast" quorum-based storage implementations are introduced. In short, "semifast" implementations allow at most one "slow" *read* per each *write* where a "slow" *read* can take more than a single round. Other *read* and all *write* operations in a "semifast" implementation must remain "fast", i.e., complete in a single round.

CHAPTER 7

Probabilistic Quorum Systems

7.1 INTRODUCTION

For modern large-scale distributed systems, including cloud computing systems, high availability is of paramount importance. Moreover, due to the sheer number of processes involved in a such a distributed system, these systems require *partition tolerance*, i.e., tolerating periods of complete disconnection between different subsets of processes while maintaining high availability. On the other hand, the celebrated CAP theorem [Brewer, 2000, Gilbert and Lynch, 2002] states that, in short, no distributed system can provide consistency, high availability and partition tolerance. Hence, the mentioned large scale distributed systems often relax consistency guarantees only to provide eventual consistency [Vogels, 2009].

As we already discussed in depth, the defining point of quorum systems is consistency. Moreover, quorum systems aim at providing high availability (Sec. 3.3.2). However, this implies that quorum systems cannot guarantee partition tolerance — this is fairly intuitive from the requirement for the non-empty quorum intersections. Furthermore, limited availability of classical, strongly consistent, quorum systems is known to be an issue for a long time [Wool, 1998]. Recall here (Chapter 3, Section 3.3.2) that, for any quorum system $\boldsymbol{QS}$: (a) the resilience $\mathcal{R}(\boldsymbol{QS})$ is at most $\left\lfloor \frac{n-1}{2} \right\rfloor$ (where n is the number of nodes in the system); and (b) the failure probability $F_p(\boldsymbol{QS})$ tends to 1 when the individual failure probability p is greater than $1/2$.

With a seemingly limited applicability of classical quorum systems in meeting the large-scale distributed computing demands, the natural question that arises is: How do quorum systems fit into the modern large scale distributed systems picture? Did quorum systems become obsolete?

The answer to the first question is twofold. First, systems that rely on eventual consistency must provide consistency, albeit only eventually, when a partition in the system is repaired. To achieve this, these systems resort to some quorum systems even if only eventually. The last point also gives a negative answer to the second question above.

Second, theoretical research on quorum systems had evolved in the direction of improving limited availability and partition tolerance of quorum systems well before the inception of cloud computing. This evolution went in direction of *relaxation* of the classical quorum Intersection property, to allow for *probabilistic* intersections. Today, different families of *probabilistic quorum systems* are known. In this chapter, we briefly overview some of the most fundamental families of probabilistic quorum systems, and argue how they improve availability and partition tolerance of classical quorum systems (hereafter referred to as *strict* quorum systems).

In particular, we highlight the ϵ*-intersecting* quorum systems [Malkhi et al., 2001], and its variant that extend strict Byzantine quorum systems. Finally, in Sec. 7.4 we briefly overview more recent work on highly available probabilistic quorum systems.

7.2 ϵ-INTERSECTING QUORUM SYSTEMS

The pioneer work in the context of probabilistic quorum systems was [Malkhi et al., 2001] that introduced ϵ*-intersecting* quorum systems. ϵ*-intersecting* quorum systems involve a subtle refinement of the Intersection property of classical quorum systems that allows non-intersection with a certain probability ϵ. While, strictly speaking, probabilistic quorum systems are not strict quorum systems (for they may violate the Intersection property), we continue, with slight abuse of terminology, to refer to elements of such non-strict quorum systems as quorums.

More specifically, ϵ-intersecting quorum systems are defined as follows.

Definition 7.1 **ϵ-intersecting Quorum System** Given a set $S = \{s_1, s_2 \dots s_n\}$ $(n \geq 1)$, let $\boldsymbol{\epsilon IQS}$ be a set system and let σ be a strategy for $\boldsymbol{\epsilon IQS}$ with an associated probability ϵ_σ. Then, a tuple $\langle \boldsymbol{\epsilon IQS}, \sigma \rangle$ is an ϵ-intersecting quorum system over S if and only if

(ϵ-intersection) $\forall Q_1, Q_2 \in \boldsymbol{\epsilon IQS} : P(Q_1 \cap Q_2 \neq \emptyset) \geq 1 - \epsilon_\sigma$.

The first observation to be made around Definition 7.1 is that ϵ-intersecting quorum systems couple a given set system with a specific strategy, unlike strict quorum systems.

While ϵ-intersecting quorum systems cannot guarantee consistency, they can, often transparently, substitute classical quorums in existing implementation if strong consistency is not mandatory. For example, ϵ-intersecting quorum systems can transparently used in place of strict ones in ABD (Sec. 4.1) to obtain a variant of a MWMR atomic storage implementation that violates atomicity with a certain probability. If remove the Timestamp synchronization phase from ABD *write* and the Writeback phase from ABD *read*, we obtain [Malkhi et al., 2001] a simple regular single-writer multi-reader storage implementation in which both read and write access a given probabilistic quorum only once. As expected, such an implementation violates consistency (regularity) with probability ϵ_σ [Malkhi et al., 2001].

The load of an ϵ-intersecting quorum system $\langle \boldsymbol{\epsilon IQS}, \sigma \rangle$ is simply the load induced by strategy σ on ϵ**IQS**.

Definition 7.2 **Load** Let $\langle \boldsymbol{\epsilon IQS}, \sigma \rangle$ be an ϵ-intersecting quorum system. Then, the load on $\langle \boldsymbol{\epsilon IQS}, \sigma \rangle$ is $\mathcal{L}(\langle \epsilon \mathbf{IQS}, \sigma \rangle) = \mathcal{L}_\sigma(\epsilon \mathbf{IQS})$.

The lower bound on strict quorum systems load (Theorem 3.18) can be simply generalized to obtain the following lower bound on the load of an ϵ-intersecting quorum system.

Theorem 7.3 Let $E_\sigma[|Q|]$ be an expectation of accessed quorum size for quorums $Q \in \epsilon\mathbf{IQS}$ taken over strategy σ, i.e., $E_\sigma[|Q|] = \sum_{Q_j \in \mathbf{QS}} \sigma_j |Q_j|$. Then,

$$\mathcal{L}(\langle \boldsymbol{\epsilon I\,QS}, \sigma \rangle) \geq \max \left\{ \frac{1 - \sqrt{\epsilon_\sigma}}{E_\sigma[|Q|]}, \frac{E_\sigma[|Q|]}{n} \right\}.$$

Corollary 7.4 $\mathcal{L}(\langle \epsilon\mathbf{IQS}, \sigma \rangle) \geq \frac{1-\sqrt{\epsilon_\sigma}}{\sqrt{n}}$.

Clearly, with ϵ_σ small, ϵ-intersecting quorum systems provide marginally better load than classical quorum systems, in general. However, ϵ-intersecting quorum system allow construction of quorum systems that combine both (close to) optimal load and $\Omega(n)$ resilience, something not possible with strict quorum systems. We demonstrate this later on the concrete example of an ϵ-intersecting quorum systems; before coming to this example, we revise the definitions of resilience and fault-tolerance to make them more suitable in the context of probabilistic intersections.

Namely, the issue in directly using the strict quorum systems definitions of resilience and failure probability (Definitions 3.22 and 3.25, respectively) in the context of ϵ-intersecting quorum systems, is that these definitions become biased with respect to quorums that intersect few other quorums but are very rarely used by the given strategy σ. To maintain their relevance, Definitions 3.22 and 3.25 need to be adapted in order to consider those quorums that intersect with others with very high probability. In the following, probabilities and expectations are implicitly taken with respect to strategy σ.

Definition 7.5 δ-high quality quorums Let $\langle \boldsymbol{\epsilon I\,QS}, \sigma \rangle$ be an ϵ-intersecting quorum system, and let δ be a given probability. The subset $\boldsymbol{\delta\epsilon I\,QS}$ (called δ-high quality quorums) of $\boldsymbol{\epsilon I\,QS}$ is defined as:

$$\boldsymbol{\delta\epsilon I\,QS} = \{Q \in \boldsymbol{\epsilon I\,QS} : P(Q \cap Q' \neq \emptyset) \geq 1 - \delta\},$$

where quorum $Q' \in \boldsymbol{\epsilon I\,QS}$ is chosen according to σ.

The following Lemma shows gives the probability that a quorum in an ϵ-intersecting quorum system is a δ-high quality quorum.

Lemma 7.6 $P(Q \in \boldsymbol{\delta\epsilon I\,QS}) \geq 1 - \frac{\epsilon}{\delta}$.

Proof. By Definition 7.1,

$$\epsilon \geq P(Q \cap Q' \neq \emptyset) = \sum_{Q \in \boldsymbol{\epsilon IQS}} \sigma_{\boldsymbol{\epsilon IQS}}(Q) \sum_{Q' : Q \cap Q' \neq \emptyset} \sigma_{\boldsymbol{\epsilon IQS}}(Q') \geq$$

$$\sum_{Q \notin \boldsymbol{\delta\epsilon IQS}} \sigma_{\boldsymbol{\epsilon IQS}}(Q) \sum_{Q' : Q \cap Q' \neq \emptyset} \sigma_{\boldsymbol{\epsilon IQS}}(Q') .$$

On the other hand, direct application of Definition 7.5 yields, for any fixed $Q \notin \boldsymbol{\delta\epsilon IQS}$:

$$\sum_{Q' : Q \cap Q' \neq \emptyset} \sigma_{\boldsymbol{\epsilon IQS}}(Q') = P(Q \cap Q' = \emptyset) > \delta .$$

Finally, the Lemma follows from substituting in the first inequality for δ,

$$\frac{\epsilon}{\delta} \geq \sum_{Q \notin \boldsymbol{\delta\epsilon IQS}} \sigma_{\boldsymbol{\epsilon IQS}}(Q) = 1 - P(Q \in \boldsymbol{\delta\epsilon IQS}).$$

□

Clearly, for a δ-high quality quorums to be of practically high quality, δ should be small. Choosing small δ carefully so that ϵ/δ remains small, δ-high quality quorums are good in a sense that: (a) they intersect with other quorums with high probability (by Definition 7.5), and (b) they are selected by strategy σ with high probability (by Lemma 7.6). To this end, a concrete choice for δ (with assumption that ϵ is already small) is to have $\delta = \epsilon/\delta = \sqrt{\epsilon}$. Hence, the following definition:

Definition 7.7 The set of $\sqrt{\epsilon}$-high quality quorums of $\langle \boldsymbol{\epsilon IQS}, \sigma \rangle$ are called *high quality quorums* of $\langle \boldsymbol{\epsilon IQS}, \sigma \rangle$.

Armed with Definition 7.7 we are ready to define resilience and failure probability of ϵ-intersecting quorum systems.

Definition 7.8 Resilience Let $\boldsymbol{HQ}$ be the set of high quality quorums of $\langle \boldsymbol{\epsilon IQS}, \sigma \rangle$ and let $\boldsymbol{S} = \{S \in \boldsymbol{\epsilon IQS} | S \cap Q \neq \emptyset \text{ for all } Q \in \boldsymbol{HQ}\}$. Then, the resilience $\mathcal{R}(\langle \boldsymbol{\epsilon IQS}, \sigma \rangle) = min_{S \in \boldsymbol{S}} |S|$.

Remark 7.9 Notice that the $m(\boldsymbol{QS})$ upper bound on resilience of strict quorum systems no longer applies to ϵ-intersecting quorum systems.

Definition 7.10 Failure probability Let $\boldsymbol{HQ}$ be the set of high quality quorums of $\langle \boldsymbol{\epsilon IQS}, \sigma \rangle$. Denote by $F_p(Q)$ the probability that some node in $Q \in \boldsymbol{HQ}$ fails. Then, assuming the uniform probabilistic fault model, failure probability $F_p(\langle \boldsymbol{\epsilon IQS}, \sigma \rangle)$ is defined as:

$$F_p(\langle \boldsymbol{\epsilon IQS}, \sigma \rangle) = \prod_{Q \in \mathbf{HQ}} F_p(Q).$$

Example. A concrete example of an ϵ-intersecting quorum system (denoted by $\boldsymbol{\epsilon IQS}_{l\sqrt{n}}$) demonstrating better availability of probabilistic quorum systems compared to strict ones is the one in which the quorums are all sets of size $l\sqrt{n}$, with a strategy chosen uniformly at random (denoted by σ_{rnd}), such that $\sigma_{\boldsymbol{\epsilon IQS}_{l\sqrt{n}}}(Q) = \frac{1}{|Q|}$, for all $Q \in \boldsymbol{\epsilon IQS}_{l\sqrt{n}}$. Here, constant l is chosen to make ϵ sufficiently small.

It is not difficult to show that the probability of two such probabilistic quorums have an empty intersection is:

$$P(Q \cup Q' = \emptyset) = \frac{\binom{n-l\sqrt{n}}{l\sqrt{n}}}{\binom{n}{l\sqrt{n}}} \leq e^{-l^2},$$

which makes $\langle \boldsymbol{\epsilon IQS}_{l\sqrt{n}}, \sigma_{rnd} \rangle$ an e^{-l^2}-intersecting quorum system with load of $O(1/\sqrt{n})$.

Since $\langle \boldsymbol{\epsilon IQS}_{l\sqrt{n}}, \sigma_{rnd} \rangle$ is symmetrically constructed with uniform access strategy, all its quorums are high quality quorums. Then, since $\langle \boldsymbol{\epsilon IQS}_{l\sqrt{n}}, \sigma_{rnd} \rangle$ can tolerate up to $n - l\sqrt{n}$ crashes, its resilience is higher than that of a Majority coterie, exemplifying the fact that ϵ-intersecting quorum systems can have resilience higher than strict quorum systems (notice here how the probabilistic intersection property relaxes the $m(\boldsymbol{\epsilon IQS})$.

Finally, using the Chernoff bound, it can be shown that the failure probability of $\epsilon\mathbf{IQS}_{\mathbf{l}\sqrt{\mathbf{n}}}$ is less than $e^{-\Omega(n)}$ for $p \leq 1 - \frac{l}{\sqrt{n}}$, which is asymptotically optimal and if $p \geq 1/2$ strictly better than failure probability of any strict quorum system.

7.3 (b, ϵ)-DISSEMINATION QUORUM SYSTEMS

In this section, we consider an extension of ϵ-intersecting quorum systems from crash fault model to Byzantine fault model. Namely [Malkhi et al., 2001], dissemination quorum systems can be ported to probabilistic context, to obtain (b, ϵ)-dissemination quorum systems, similarly as ϵ-intersecting quorum systems do with strict classical quorum systems.

Definition 7.11 (b, ϵ)**-dissemination Quorum Systems** Given a set $S = \{s_1, s_2 \ldots s_n\}$ $(n \geq 1)$, let $\boldsymbol{\epsilon DQS}$ be a set system and let σ be a strategy for $\boldsymbol{\epsilon DQS}$ with an associated probability ϵ_σ.

Then, given the threshold adversary $\boldsymbol{B_b}$, a tuple $\langle \boldsymbol{\epsilon DQS}, \sigma \rangle$ is an (b, ϵ)-dissemination quorum system over S if and only if the resilience of $\langle \boldsymbol{\epsilon DQS}, \sigma \rangle$ is higher than b and

$$(\epsilon\text{-Byzantine intersection})\ \forall Q_1, Q_2 \in \boldsymbol{\epsilon DQS} : P(Q_1 \cap Q_2 \notin \boldsymbol{B_b}) \geq 1 - \epsilon_\sigma .$$

A (b, ϵ)-dissemination quorum system can be directly used in place of a classical dissemination quorum system in many implementations (e.g., Phalanx of Sec. 5.1.2) to obtain an implementation variant that features better availability but probabilistically sacrifices consistency.

The most interesting feature of (b, ϵ)-dissemination quorum systems is that they abolish the upper bound on the fraction of tolerable Byzantine faults. Recall (Sec. 5.1) that strict b-dissemination quorum systems have the resilience upper bound of roughly one third of Byzantine failures. On the other hand, (b, ϵ)-dissemination quorum systems can overcome any fraction α of Byzantine faults, thus considerably improving the availability of implementations that rely on (b, ϵ)-dissemination quorum systems.

We demonstrate this by showing that, perhaps surprisingly, $\boldsymbol{\epsilon IQS}_{l\sqrt{n}}$ exemplified in Sec. 7.2 as a crash-stop ϵ-intersecting quorum satisfies the definition of (b, ϵ)-dissemination quorum system with the proper adjustment of ϵ [Malkhi et al., 2001].

Lemma 7.12 *Given adversary* $\boldsymbol{B}_{\lfloor \frac{n}{3} \rfloor}$, $\langle \boldsymbol{\epsilon IQS}_{l\sqrt{n}}, \sigma_{rnd} \rangle$ *is a* (b, ϵ)*-dissemination quorum system, with* $\epsilon = 2e^{-\frac{l^2}{6}}$.

Proof. It is sufficient to show that for any $Q_1, Q_2 \in \boldsymbol{\epsilon IQS}_{l\sqrt{n}}$ and $B \in \boldsymbol{B}_{\lfloor \frac{n}{3} \rfloor}$ $P((Q_1 \cap Q_2) \subseteq B) \leq 2e^{-\frac{l^2}{6}}$,

$$p = P((Q_1 \cap Q_2) \subseteq B) = P(|Q_1 \cap Q_2| = |Q_1 \cap Q_2 \cap B|) .$$

Summing up for all possible sizes of the above intersections, we further obtain

$$p = \sum_{i=0}^{l\sqrt{n}} P(|Q_1 \cap Q_2| = i \wedge |Q_1 \cap Q_2 \cap B| = i)$$

$$= \sum_{i=0}^{l\sqrt{n}} \frac{\binom{l\sqrt{n}}{i}\binom{n-l\sqrt{n}}{l\sqrt{n}-i}}{\binom{n}{l\sqrt{n}}} \frac{\frac{1}{2}\binom{\frac{n}{3}}{i}\binom{n-i}{l\sqrt{n}-i}\binom{n-l\sqrt{n}}{l\sqrt{n}-i}}{\frac{1}{2}\binom{n}{l\sqrt{n}}\binom{l\sqrt{n}}{i}\binom{n-l\sqrt{n}}{l\sqrt{n}-i}}$$

$$= \sum_{i=0}^{l\sqrt{n}} \frac{\binom{l\sqrt{n}}{i}\binom{n-l\sqrt{n}}{l\sqrt{n}-i}}{\binom{n}{l\sqrt{n}}} \frac{\frac{n}{3}!(n-i)!}{(\frac{n}{3}-i)!n!} \leq \sum_{i=0}^{l\sqrt{n}} \frac{\binom{l\sqrt{n}}{i}\binom{n-l\sqrt{n}}{l\sqrt{n}-i}}{\binom{n}{l\sqrt{n}}} \left(\frac{1}{3}\right)^i ;$$

then since $\frac{\binom{n-l\sqrt{n}}{l\sqrt{n}-i}}{\binom{n}{l\sqrt{n}}} \leq \left(\frac{l\sqrt{n}}{n}\right)^i \left(\frac{n-l\sqrt{n}}{n-i}\right)^{l\sqrt{n}-i}$, we have

$$p \leq \sum_{i=0}^{l\sqrt{n}} \binom{l\sqrt{n}}{i} \left(\frac{l\sqrt{n}}{n}\right)^i \left(\frac{n-l\sqrt{n}}{n-i}\right)^{l\sqrt{n}-i} \left(\frac{1}{3}\right)^i .$$

Then, since $1+x \leq e^x$ and applying additionally $\binom{l\sqrt{n}}{i}\left(\frac{l\sqrt{n}}{n}\right)^i \leq \frac{(l\sqrt{n})^i(l\sqrt{n})^i}{i!n^i}$ for $i \leq (l\sqrt{n})/6$) and $\binom{l\sqrt{n}}{i}\left(\frac{l\sqrt{n}}{n}\right)^i \left(\frac{n-l\sqrt{n}}{n-i}\right)^{l\sqrt{n}-i} \leq 1$ for $i > (l\sqrt{n})/6$), we obtain:

$$p \leq \sum_{i=0}^{l\sqrt{n}/6} \frac{(l^2)^i}{i!} e^{-\frac{(l\sqrt{n}-i)^2}{n-i}} \left(\frac{1}{3}\right)^i + \sum_{i=l\sqrt{n}/6+1}^{l\sqrt{n}} \left(\frac{1}{3}\right)^i$$

$$\leq \sum_{i=0}^{l\sqrt{n}/6} \frac{\left(\frac{l^2}{3}\right)^i}{i!} e^{-l^2\left(\frac{5}{6}\right)^2} + \sum_{i=l\sqrt{n}/6+1}^{l\sqrt{n}} \left(\frac{1}{3}\right)^i .$$

By Maclaurin series expansion for e^x we have $\sum_{i \geq 0} \frac{x^i}{i!} = e^x$, and hence we can eliminate the first sum, whereas the second sum is bounded by $3^{-\frac{l\sqrt{n}}{6}}$ by geometric series expansion. Therefore,

$$p \leq e^{-l^2\left(\frac{5}{6}\right)^2} e^{\frac{l^2}{3}} + 3^{-\frac{l\sqrt{n}}{6}} .$$

Finally, applying $e < 3$ and $l \leq \sqrt{n}$ (since $l\sqrt{n} \leq n$), we have

$$p \leq 2e^{-\frac{l^2}{6}} .$$

□

Applying similar arguments as in the proof of Lemma 7.12, it can be even shown that $\langle \boldsymbol{\epsilon I QS}_{l\sqrt{n}}, \sigma_{rnd} \rangle$ is a (b, ϵ)-dissemination quorum systems even for adversary $\boldsymbol{B}_\alpha$, where $\frac{1}{3} < \alpha < 1$ is *any* fraction of Byzantine servers, with $\epsilon = 2\alpha^{l^2\left(\frac{1-\sqrt{\alpha}}{2}\right)} \frac{1}{1-\alpha}$. These examples clearly demonstrate the availability benefits of probabilistic quorum systems over strict ones.

7.4 BIBLIOGRAPHIC NOTES

- Besides the probabilistic quorum variants presented here, [Malkhi et al., 2001] also defines (b, ϵ)-masking quorum systems with a more detailed exposition presented in [Malkhi et al., 1998]. [Merideth and Reiter, 2007] complement this work by analyzing probabilistic intersections in the context of opaque masking quorum systems.

- One issue with ϵ-intersecting quorum systems is that they do not account for the network adversary that controls the system scheduler in, e.g., asynchronous system. Intuitively, such an adversary could always violate the probabilistic intersection guarantees by, e.g., partitioning the writer and the reader and two quorums eQ_1 and eQ_2 by arbitrarily delaying messages sent by the writer to nodes in eQ_2 and by the reader to eQ_1.

  [Yu, 2006] explicitly acknowledges this issue, and proposes an alternative definition of probabilistic quorum systems, called *signed* quorum systems. Signed quorum system are not defined around access strategies (for these can be disturbed by the scheduler); in the approach of [Yu, 2006], a strategy is implicit and dictated by the scheduler and failures in the system. In short, signed quorum systems allow both positive and negative node IDs in a quorum, where negative IDs denote nodes that are suspected to be faulty and cannot be accessed.[1] Signed quorum systems require quorums to intersect, *or* non-intersecting quorums to differ in at least 2α node states (signs) for some integer α. The probability of having an empty intersection between two quorums is then the probability that two clients assess at least 2α nodes in different states which is lower for larger values of α.

- [Aiyer et al., 2005] argue that the approach of [Yu, 2006] remains vulnerable to the adversarial scheduler issue and propose k-quorum protocols to boost availability of classical quorum systems. In short, k-quorum protocols use classical quorum systems yet allow the writer to lazily contact the writer quorum such that all nodes from a quorum are contacted during $k \geq 1$ consecutive writes (vs. $k = 1$ in the classical approach), which allows the reader to return one of the last $k \geq 1$ written values.

- [Abraham and Malkhi, 2005] considers probabilistic quorum systems in the dynamic setting, proposing scalable techniques for probabilistic dynamic quorum systems. Moreover, Timed Quorum Systems [Gramoli and Raynal, 2007] extend the notion of probabilistic dynamic quorum systems to account for timing constraints related to dynamic membership changes.

[1] In other words, signed quorum systems assume a failure detector [Chandra and Toueg, 1996].

Bibliography

Michael Abd-El-Malek, Gregory R. Ganger, Garth R. Goodson, Michael K. Reiter, and Jay J. Wylie. Fault-scalable Byzantine fault-tolerant services. In *Proceedings of the 20th ACM symposium on Operating systems principles*, pages 59–74, October 2005. ISBN 1-59593-079-5. DOI: 10.1145/1095809.1095817 Cited on page(s) 81, 88

Ittai Abraham and Dahlia Malkhi. Probabilistic quorums for dynamic systems. *Distributed Computing*, 18(2):113–124, 2005. DOI: 10.1007/s00446-005-0139-2 Cited on page(s) 116

Ittai Abraham, Gregory V. Chockler, Idit Keidar, and Dahlia Malkhi. Byzantine disk paxos: optimal resilience with Byzantine shared memory. *Distributed Computing*, 18(5):387–408, 2006. DOI: 10.1007/s00446-005-0151-6 Cited on page(s) 79, 80, 87

Ittai Abraham, Gregory Chockler, Idit Keidar, and Dahlia Malkhi. Wait-free regular storage from Byzantine components. *Inf. Process. Lett.*, 101(2):60–65, 2007. DOI: 10.1016/j.ipl.2006.07.012 Cited on page(s) 79

D. Agrawal and A. El Abbadi. Efficient solution to the distributed mutual exclusion problem. In *Proceedings of the 8th annual ACM Symposium on Principles of distributed computing*, pages 193–200, New York, NY, USA, 1989. ACM. ISBN 0-89791-326-4. DOI: 10.1145/72981.72994 Cited on page(s) 2

Marcos Kawazoe Aguilera, Idit Keidar, Dahlia Malkhi, and Alexander Shraer. Dynamic atomic storage without consensus. *J. ACM*, 58(2):7, 2011. DOI: 10.1145/1944345.1944348 Cited on page(s) 49

Amitanand S. Aiyer, Lorenzo Alvisi, and Rida A. Bazzi. On the availability of non-strict quorum systems. In *Proceedings of the 19th International Conference on Distributed Computing*, pages 48–62, 2005. Cited on page(s) 116

Amitanand S. Aiyer, Lorenzo Alvisi, and Rida A. Bazzi. Bounded wait-free implementation of optimally resilient Byzantine storage without (unproven) cryptographic assumptions. In *Proceedings of the 21st International Symposium on Distributed Computing*, pages 7–19, September 2007. DOI: 10.1145/1281100.1281147 Cited on page(s) 79

Jeannie R. Albrecht and Yasushi Saito. Rambo for dummies. Technical Report HPL-2005-39, HP Laboratories Palo Alto, February 2005. Cited on page(s) 49

Bowen Alpern and Fred B. Schneider. Defining liveness. *Inf. Process. Lett.*, 21(4):181–185, 1985. DOI: 10.1016/0020-0190(85)90056-0 Cited on page(s) 10

Y. Amir, L. E. Moser, P. M. Melliar-Smith, D. A. Agarwal, and P. Ciarfella. The totem single-ring ordering and membership protocol. *ACM Trans. Comput. Syst.*, 13(4):311–342, 1995. ISSN 0734-2071. DOI: 10.1145/210223.210224 Cited on page(s) 2

Hagit Attiya. Robust simulation of shared memory: 20 years after. *Bulletin of the European Association for Theoretical Computer Science EATCS*, (100):99–113, Feb 2010. Cited on page(s) 47

Hagit Attiya and Jennifer Welch. *Distributed Computing. Fundamentals, Simulations, and Advanced Topics*. McGraw-Hill, 1998. Cited on page(s) 5

Hagit Attiya, Amotz Bar-Noy, and Danny Dolev. Sharing memory robustly in message-passing systems. *J. ACM*, 42(1):124–142, 1995. DOI: 10.1145/200836.200869 Cited on page(s) 2, 25, 29, 47

Daniel Barbara and Hector Garcia-Molina. The vulnerability of vote assignments. *ACM Trans. Comput. Syst.*, 4(3):187–213, 1986. ISSN 0734-2071. DOI: 10.1145/6420.6421 Cited on page(s) 2, 22

Rida Bazzi and Yin Ding. Non-skipping timestamps for Byzantine data storage systems. In *Proceedings of the 18th International Symposium on Distributed Computing*, pages 405–419, Oct 2004. DOI: 10.1007/978-3-540-30186-8_29 Cited on page(s) 79

Rida A. Bazzi. Planar quorums. *Theor. Comput. Sci.*, 243(1-2):243–268, 2000a. ISSN 0304-3975. DOI: 10.1016/S0304-3975(98)00208-4 Cited on page(s) 23

Rida A. Bazzi. Synchronous Byzantine quorum systems. *Distrib. Comput.*, 13(1):45–52, 2000b. ISSN 0178-2770. DOI: 10.1007/s004460050004 Cited on page(s) 79

Rida A. Bazzi. Access cost for asynchronous Byzantine quorum systems. *Distributed Computing*, 14 (1):41–48, 2001. DOI: 10.1007/PL00008925 Cited on page(s) 22, 80

Kenneth P. Birman and Robert V. Renesse. *Reliable Distributed Computing with the ISIS Toolkit*. IEEE Computer Society Press, Los Alamitos, CA, USA, 1994. ISBN 0818653426. Cited on page(s) 2

Romain Boichat, Partha Dutta, Svend Frölund, and Rachid Guerraoui. Deconstructing Paxos. *SIGACT News in Distributed Computing*, 34(1):47–67, 2003. ISSN 0163-5700. DOI: 10.1145/637437.637447 Cited on page(s) 31, 49

Francisco Vilar Brasileiro, Fabíola Greve, Achour Mostéfaoui, and Michel Raynal. Consensus in one communication step. In *Proceedings of the 6th International Parallel Computing Technologies Conference*, pages 42–50, 2001. Cited on page(s) 107

Eric A. Brewer. Towards robust distributed systems (abstract). In *Proceedings of The 19th Annual ACM Symposium on Principles of Distributed Computing*, page 7, 2000. ISBN 1-58113-183-6. Cited on page(s) 109

Christian Cachin, Rachid Guerraoui, and Luís Rodrigues. *Introduction to Reliable and Secure Distributed Programming*. Springer-Verlag, 2011. DOI: 10.1007/978-3-642-15260-3 Cited on page(s) 5, 13

Miguel Castro and Barbara Liskov. Practical Byzantine fault tolerance and proactive recovery. *ACM Trans. Comput. Syst.*, 20(4):398–461, 2002. ISSN 0734-2071. DOI: 10.1145/571637.571640 Cited on page(s) 52, 59, 79

Tushar Chandra and Sam Toueg. Unreliable failure detectors for reliable distributed systems. Technical Report TR95-1535, Cornell University, Computer Science Department, August 1995. DOI: 10.1145/226643.226647 Cited on page(s) 12

Tushar Deepak Chandra and Sam Toueg. Unreliable failure detectors for reliable distributed systems. 43(2):225–267, March 1996. DOI: 10.1145/226643.226647 Cited on page(s) 116

S. Y. Cheung, M. H. Ammar, and M. Ahamad. The grid protocol: A high performance scheme for maintaining replicated data. *IEEE Trans. on Knowl. and Data Eng.*, 4(6):582–592, 1992. ISSN 1041-4347. DOI: 10.1109/69.180609 Cited on page(s) 24

James Cowling, Daniel Myers, Barbara Liskov, Rodrigo Rodrigues, and Liuba Shrira. HQ replication: A hybrid quorum protocol for Byzantine fault tolerance. In *Proceedings of the 7th Symposium on Operating Systems Design and Implementations*, pages 177–190, November 2006. Cited on page(s) 79

Susan B. Davidson, Hector Garcia-Molina, and Dale Skeen. Consistency in a partitioned network: a survey. *ACM Comput. Surv.*, 17(3):341–370, 1985. ISSN 0360-0300. DOI: 10.1145/5505.5508 Cited on page(s) 23

Partha Dutta, Rachid Guerraoui, Ron R. Levy, and Marko Vukolic. Fast access to distributed atomic memory. *SIAM J. Comput.*, 39(8):3752–3783, 2010. DOI: 10.1137/090757010 Cited on page(s) 107, 108

Cynthia Dwork, Nancy A. Lynch, and Larry J. Stockmeyer. Consensus in the presence of partial synchrony. *J. ACM*, 35(2):288–323, 1988. DOI: 10.1145/42282.42283 Cited on page(s) 8

Burkhard Englert and Alexander A. Shvartsman. Graceful quorum reconfiguration in a robust emulation of shared memory. In *Proceedings of the 20th International Conference on Distributed Computing Systems*, pages 454–463, 2000. DOI: 10.1109/ICDCS.2000.840958 Cited on page(s) 49

Michael J. Fischer, Nancy A. Lynch, and Michael S. Paterson. Impossibility of distributed consensus with one faulty process. *Journal of the ACM*, 32(2):374–382, April 1985. DOI: 10.1145/3149.214121 Cited on page(s) 12, 31, 49

Hector Garcia-Molina and Daniel Barbara. How to assign votes in a distributed system. *J. ACM*, 32(4):841–860, 1985. ISSN 0004-5411. DOI: 10.1145/4221.4223 Cited on page(s) 16

Chryssis Georgiou, Nicolas C. Nicolaou, and Alexander A. Shvartsman. Fault-tolerant semifast implementations of atomic read/write registers. *J. Parallel Distrib. Comput.*, 69(1):62–79, 2009. DOI: 10.1016/j.jpdc.2008.05.004 Cited on page(s) 108

David K. Gifford. Weighted voting for replicated data. In *Proceedings of the 7th ACM symposium on Operating systems principles*, pages 150–162, December 1979. ISBN 0-89791-009-5. DOI: 10.1145/800215.806583 Cited on page(s) 2, 16

Seth Gilbert and Nancy Lynch. Brewer's conjecture and the feasibility of consistent, available, partition-tolerant web services. *SIGACT News*, 33(2):51–59, 2002. ISSN 0163-5700. DOI: 10.1145/564585.564601 Cited on page(s) 109

Seth Gilbert, Nancy A. Lynch, and Alexander A. Shvartsman. Rambo ii: Rapidly reconfigurable atomic memory for dynamic networks. In *Proceedings of the 2003 International Conference on Dependable Systems and Networks*, pages 259–268, 2003. DOI: 10.1109/DSN.2003.1209936 Cited on page(s) 49

Seth Gilbert, Nancy A. Lynch, and Alexander A. Shvartsman. Rambo: a robust, reconfigurable atomic memory service for dynamic networks. *Distributed Computing*, 23(4):225–272, 2010. DOI: 10.1007/s00446-010-0117-1 Cited on page(s) 25, 36, 39, 49

Garth Goodson, Jay Wylie, Gregory Ganger, and Michael Reiter. Efficient Byzantine-tolerant erasure-coded storage. In *Proceedings of the International Conference on Dependable Systems and Networks*, pages 135–144, 2004. DOI: 10.1109/DSN.2004.1311884 Cited on page(s) 81

Vincent Gramoli and Michel Raynal. Timed quorum systems for large-scale and dynamic environments. In *Proceedings of the 11th International Conference on Principles of Distributed Systems*, pages 429–442, 2007. Cited on page(s) 116

Rachid Guerraoui and Marko Vukolić. How Fast Can a Very Robust Read Be? In *Proceedings of the 25th ACM Symposium on Principles of Distributed Computing*, pages 248–257, July 2006. DOI: 10.1145/1146381.1146419 Cited on page(s) 79, 80

Rachid Guerraoui and Marko Vukolić. Refined quorum systems. *Distributed Computing*, 2010. http://dx.doi.org/10.1007/s00446-010-0103-7. DOI: 10.1007/s00446-010-0103-7 Cited on page(s) 79, 82, 91, 98, 107

Rachid Guerraoui, Ron R. Levy, and Marko Vukolić. Lucky read/write access to robust atomic storage. In *Proceedings of the International Conference on Dependable Systems and Networks*, pages 125–136, June 2006. ISBN 0-7695-2607-1. DOI: 10.1109/DSN.2006.50 Cited on page(s) 81

Rachid Guerraoui, Nikola Knežević, Vivien Quéma, and Marko Vukolić. The next 700 BFT protocols. In *Proceedings of the 5th ACM SIGOPS/EuroSys European Conference on Computer Systems*, pages 363–376, 2010. DOI: 10.1145/1755913.1755950 Cited on page(s) 81

Maurice Herlihy. A quorum-consensus replication method for abstract data types. *ACM Trans. Comput. Syst.*, 4(1):32–53, 1986. ISSN 0734-2071. DOI: 10.1145/6306.6308 Cited on page(s) 2

Maurice Herlihy. Wait-free synchronization. *ACM Transactions on Programming Languages and Systems*, 13(1):124–149, January 1991. DOI: 10.1145/114005.102808 Cited on page(s) 10

Martin Hirt and Ueli M. Maurer. Player simulation and general adversary structures in perfect multiparty computation. *J. Cryptology*, 13(1):31–60, 2000. DOI: 10.1007/s001459910003 Cited on page(s) 52

Ron Holzman, Yosi Marcus, and David Peleg. Load balancing in quorum systems. *SIAM J. Discret. Math.*, 10(2):223–245, 1997. ISSN 0895-4801. DOI: 10.1137/S0895480193260303 Cited on page(s) 2

Prasad Jayanti, Tushar Deepak Chandra, and Sam Toueg. Fault-tolerant wait-free shared objects. *Journal of the ACM*, 45(3):451–500, 1998. ISSN 0004-5411. DOI: 10.1145/278298.278305 Cited on page(s) 6, 77

Ramakrishna Kotla, Lorenzo Alvisi, Mike Dahlin, Allen Clement, and Edmund Wong. Zyzzyva: Speculative Byzantine fault tolerance. *ACM Trans. Comput. Syst.*, 27(4):1–39, 2009. ISSN 0734-2071. DOI: 10.1145/1323293.1294267 Cited on page(s) 81, 88, 107

Leslie Lamport. Time, clocks, and the ordering of events in a distributed system. *Commun. ACM*, 21(7):558–565, 1978a. DOI: 10.1145/359545.359563 Cited on page(s) 1, 2

Leslie Lamport. The implementation of reliable distributed multiprocess systems. *Computer Networks*, 2:95–114, 1978b. DOI: 10.1016/0376-5075(78)90045-4 Cited on page(s) 1

Leslie Lamport. On interprocess communication. *Distributed computing*, 1(1):77–101, May 1986. DOI: 10.1007/BF01786227 Cited on page(s) 9, 10

Leslie Lamport. The part-time parliament. *ACM Transactions on Computer Systems*, 16(2):133–169, 1998. ISSN 0734-2071. DOI: 10.1145/279227.279229 Cited on page(s) 12, 25, 31, 32, 47

Leslie Lamport. Paxos made simple. *ACM SIGACT news distributed computing column*, 32(4):51–58, 2001. ISSN 0163-5700. Cited on page(s) 31, 32, 47

Leslie Lamport. Lower bounds for asynchronous consensus. *Future Directions in Distributed Computing*, pages 22–23, May 2003. DOI: 10.1007/3-540-37795-6_5 Cited on page(s) 107

Leslie Lamport. Fast Paxos. *Distributed Computing*, 19(2):79–103, 2006. DOI: 10.1007/s00446-006-0005-x Cited on page(s) 81, 82, 85, 91, 97, 107

Leslie Lamport, Robert Shostak, and Marshall Pease. The Byzantine generals problem. *ACM Trans. Program. Lang. Syst.*, 4(3):382–401, 1982a. ISSN 0164-0925. DOI: 10.1145/357172.357176 Cited on page(s) 51, 77

Leslie Lamport, Robert E. Shostak, and Marshall C. Pease. The Byzantine generals problem. *ACM Trans. Program. Lang. Syst.*, 4(3):382–401, 1982b. DOI: 10.1145/357172.357176 Cited on page(s) 6

Nancy A. Lynch. *Distributed Algorithms*. Morgan-Kaufmann, 1996. Cited on page(s) 5, 11

Nancy A. Lynch and Alexander A. Shvartsman. Robust emulation of shared memory using dynamic quorum-acknowledged broadcasts. In *Proceedings of the 27th Annual International Symposium on Fault-Tolerant Computing*, pages 272–281, 1997. DOI: 10.1109/FTCS.1997.614100 Cited on page(s) 49

Nancy A. Lynch and Alexander A. Shvartsman. Rambo: A reconfigurable atomic memory service for dynamic networks. In *Proceedings of the 16th International Conference on Distributed Computing*, pages 173–190, 2002. Cited on page(s) 49

Nancy A. Lynch and Mark R. Tuttle. An introduction to input/output automata. *CWI Quarterly*, 2 (3):219–246, 1989. Cited on page(s) 5, 49

M. Maekawa. A $\sqrt{N}$ algorithm for mutual exclusion in decentralized systems. *ACM Trans. Comput. Syst.*, 3(2):145–159, 1985. DOI: 10.1145/214438.214445 Cited on page(s) 2, 23

Dahlia Malkhi. *Quorum Systems. The Encyclopedia of Distributed Computing*, J. Urban and P. Dasgupta, eds., Kluwer Academic, 2000. Cited on page(s) 17, 23

Dahlia Malkhi and Michael Reiter. Byzantine quorum systems. *Distributed Computing*, 11(4):203–213, 1998a. ISSN 0178-2770. DOI: 10.1007/s004460050050 Cited on page(s) 2, 52, 56, 67, 68, 72, 75, 77, 79

Dahlia Malkhi and Michael K. Reiter. Secure and scalable replication in phalanx. In *Proceedings of the 17th Symposium on Reliable Distributed Systems*, pages 51–58, 1998b. URL `citeseer.ist.psu.edu/article/malkhi98secure.html`. Cited on page(s) 52, 79

Dahlia Malkhi, Michael Reiter, Avishai Wool, and Rebecca N. Wright. Probabilistic byzantine quorum systems. In *Proceedings of the seventeenth annual ACM symposium on Principles of distributed computing*, PODC '98, pages 321–, New York, NY, USA, 1998. ACM. ISBN 0-89791-977-7.

URL http://doi.acm.org/10.1145/277697.277781. DOI: 10.1145/277697.277781 Cited on page(s) 115

Dahlia Malkhi, Michael K. Reiter, and Avishai Wool. The load and availability of Byzantine quorum systems. *SIAM J. Comput.*, 29(6):1889–1906, 2000. ISSN 0097-5397. DOI: 10.1137/S0097539797325235 Cited on page(s) 55, 79

Dahlia Malkhi, Michael Reiter, Avishai Wool, and Rebecca Wright. Probabilistic quorum systems. *Inf. Comput.*, 170(2):184–206, 2001. DOI: 10.1006/inco.2001.3054 Cited on page(s) 110, 113, 114, 115

J-P. Martin, L. Alvisi, and M. Dahlin. Small Byzantine quorum systems. In *Proceedings of the International Conference on Dependable Systems and Networks*, pages 374–383, June 2002a. URL http://www.cs.utexas.edu/users/jpmartin/papers/smallByz_DSN.ps. DOI: 10.1109/DSN.2002.1028922 Cited on page(s) 79

Jean-Philippe Martin and Lorenzo Alvisi. Fast Byzantine consensus. *IEEE Trans. Dependable Secur. Comput.*, 3(3):202–215, 2006. ISSN 1545-5971. DOI: 10.1109/TDSC.2006.35 Cited on page(s) 81, 88, 107

Jean-Philippe Martin, Lorenzo Alvisi, and Michael Dahlin. Minimal Byzantine storage. In *Proceedings of the 16th International Conference on Distributed Computing*, pages 311–325, October 2002b. ISBN 3-540-00073-9. DOI: 10.1007/3-540-36108-1_21 Cited on page(s) 79

Michael G. Merideth and Michael K. Reiter. Probabilistic opaque quorum systems. In *Proceedings of the 21st International Conference on Distributed Computing*, pages 403–419, 2007. Cited on page(s) 115

Moni Naor and Udi Wieder. Scalable and dynamic quorum systems. *Distributed Computing*, 17(4): 311–322, 2005. DOI: 10.1007/s00446-004-0114-3 Cited on page(s) 49

Moni Naor and Avishai Wool. The load, capacity, and availability of quorum systems. *SIAM J. Comput.*, 27(2):423–447, 1998. ISSN 0097-5397. DOI: 10.1137/S0097539795281232 Cited on page(s) 2, 19, 20, 21, 23, 24

Brian M. Oki and Barbara H. Liskov. Viewstamped replication: A new primary copy method to support highly-available distributed systems. In *Proceedings of the seventh annual ACM Symposium on Principles of distributed computing*, PODC '88, pages 8–17, New York, NY, USA, 1988. ACM. ISBN 0-89791-277-2. URL http://doi.acm.org/10.1145/62546.62549. DOI: 10.1145/62546.62549 Cited on page(s) 47

Christos H. Papadimitriou and Kenneth Steiglitz. *Combinatorial optimization: algorithms and complexity*. Prentice-Hall, Inc., Upper Saddle River, NJ, USA, 1982. ISBN 0-13-152462-3. Cited on page(s) 20

David Peleg and Avishai Wool. The availability of quorum systems. *Inf. Comput.*, 123(2):210–223, 1995. ISSN 0890-5401. DOI: 10.1006/inco.1995.1169 Cited on page(s) 22, 23, 24

David Peleg and Avishai Wool. Crumbling walls: A class of practical and efficient quorum systems. *Distributed Computing*, 10(2):87–97, 1997. DOI: 10.1007/s004460050027 Cited on page(s) 23

Gary L. Peterson and Michael J. Fischer. Economical solutions for the critical section problem in a distributed system (extended abstract). In *Proceedings of the 9th Annual ACM Symposium on Theory of Computing*, pages 91–97, 1977. DOI: 10.1145/800105.803398 Cited on page(s) 9

HariGovind V. Ramasamy and Christian Cachin. Parsimonious asynchronous Byzantine-fault-tolerant atomic broadcast. In *Proceedings of the 9th International Conference on Principles of Distributed Systems*, pages 88–102, December 2005. DOI: 10.1007/11795490_9 Cited on page(s) 81

Michel Raynal. *Communication and Agreement Abstractions for Fault-tolerant Asynchronous Distributed Systems*. Morgan and Claypool Publishers, 1st edition, 2010. ISBN 160845293X, 9781608452934. DOI: 10.2200/S00236ED1V01Y201004DCT002 Cited on page(s) 12, 13

Rodrigo Rodrigues, Petr Kouznetsov, and Bobby Bhattacharjee. Large-scale Byzantine fault tolerance: safe but not always live. In *Proceedings of the 3rd workshop on on Hot Topics in System Dependability*, page 17, Berkeley, CA, USA, 2007. USENIX Association. Cited on page(s) 53

Robert H. Thomas. A majority consensus approach to concurrency control for multiple copy databases. *ACM Trans. Database Syst.*, 4(2):180–209, 1979. ISSN 0362-5915. DOI: 10.1145/320071.320076 Cited on page(s) 1, 2

Werner Vogels. Eventually consistent. *Commun. ACM*, 52(1):40–44, 2009. ISSN 0001-0782. DOI: 10.1145/1435417.1435432 Cited on page(s) 109

Marko Vukolić. The origin of quorum systems. *Bulletin of the European Association for Theoretical Computer Science EATCS*, (101):125–147, June 2010. Cited on page(s) 3

Avishai Wool. Quorum systems in replicated databases: Science or fiction? *Bulletin of the IEEE Technical Committee on Data Engineering*, 21:3–11, 1998. Cited on page(s) 109

Haifeng Yu. Signed quorum systems. *Distributed Computing*, 18(4):307–323, 2006. DOI: 10.1007/s00446-005-0133-8 Cited on page(s) 116

Piotr Zielinski. Optimistically terminating consensus: All asynchronous consensus protocols in one framework. In *Proceedings of The 5th International Symposium on Parallel and Distributed Computing*, pages 24–33, 2006. ISBN 0-7695-2638-1. DOI: 10.1109/ISPDC.2006.37 Cited on page(s) 81, 97, 107

Author's Biography

MARKO VUKOLIĆ

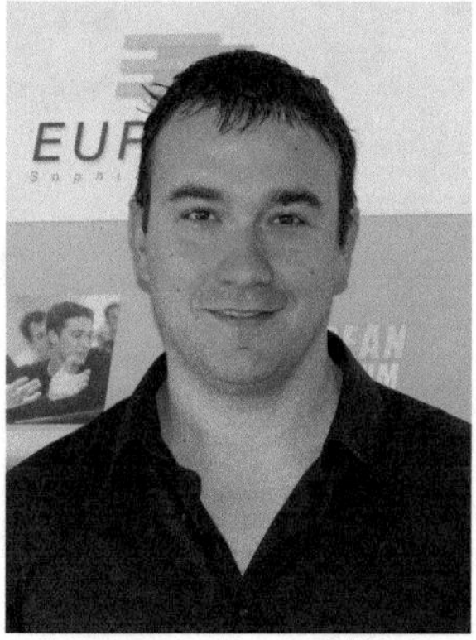

Marko Vukolić is an assistant professor in the Networking and Security Department at Eurécom, France. He received his engineering degree in Communication Systems from University of Belgrade, Serbia in 2001 and his doctor of science degree in Distributed Systems from EPFL, Switzerland in 2008. He was affiliated with IBM Research – Zurich where he spent time in the Storage Systems group as a post-doc from 2008–2010.

Index

k-quorum protocols, 116

acceptors, 12, 31, 59
adversary, 51, 52, 59, 68, 69, 74, 75, 77, 82, 87
  monotone, 51
  network, 116
  structure, 52
  threshold, 52, 54, 114
algorithm, 5
asynchronous model, 8, 25
  synchronous periods, 8, 84
atomicity, 6
Attiya, Hagit, 25
availability, 2, 3, 18, 52, 79, 109, 114

ballot, 33, 59, 92
Bar-Noy, Amotz, 25

CAP theorem, 109
capacity, 21
Castro, Miguel, 59
Chandra, Tushar, 77
channels, 6
  reliable, 8
  secure, 7
Chernoff bound, 113
cloud computing, 109
concurrency, 2, 81
consensus, 3, 12, 25, 82
  Agreement, 12, 31, 35, 59, 65
  FLP impossibility, 12, 31, 49
  obstruction-free, 31, 91
  Obstruction-free termination, 31, 35, 97
  Termination, 12, 31, 59, 97
  Validity, 12, 31, 35, 59
consensus emulation
  CL, 52, 59–67
  FastSynod, 91–98
  Synod, 25, 31–36, 59, 81, 91
consistency, 1, 21, 28, 33, 109, 110, 114
  eventual, 109
  O-Byzantine, 75, 76
  O-Stale, 75–77
coterie, 16, 53, 69
  dominated, 16
  Majority, 17, 22
  non-dominated, 16

digital signatures, 7, 56, 59, 72
  unforgeability, 7, 58, 67
  validity, 7
distributed system, 5
Dolev, Danny, 25
dynamic membership, 5, 36

eventually synchronous model, 8, 12
execution, 5
  extension, 5
  history, 10
  partial, 5
  well-formed, 10, 31
exponential backoff, 65

fail-prone set, 52

failure detector, 12, 116
  eventual leader, 12, 25, 31, 59, 65
failure probability, 21–23, 109, 111
  ϵ-intersecting, 113
fast protocols, 81, 82, 84, 87
  semifast, 108
fast quorums, 82
fault model
  authenticated Byzantine, 7, 56, 59, 74, 79
  crash, 6, 25, 26, 91, 98
  probabilistic, 8
  unauthenticated Byzantine, 7, 67, 68, 72, 77, 82, 84, 87, 91, 98
  uniform probabilistic, 8, 22, 113
fault-configuration, 7
fault-tolerance, 2, 22, 111
faults, 6
  Byzantine, 6, 51, 59
  crash, 6, 84, 98

geometric series, 115
Gilbert, Seth, 36
global clock, 8
gossiping, 42
graceful degradation, 84
group communication, 2
Guerraoui, Rachid, 98

high quality quorums, 112, 113

I/O automaton, 5
intersection
  ϵ, 110
  ϵ-Byzantine, 114
  asymmetric, 2, 16
  Byzantine, 52, 65, 67, 83, 102, 104
  Class-1, 82, 84, 85, 89, 96, 104
  Class-2, 83, 84, 86, 88–90
  Class-3, 83, 84, 89
  M-Byzantine, 68, 74
  Minimality, 16
  non-empty, 1, 3, 15, 22, 28, 31, 51, 109
  probabilistic, 109–111, 113

Jayanti, Prasad, 77

Lamport, Leslie, 31, 91
latency, 9, 29, 98
  common-case, 9, 10, 81, 98
  worst-case, 69, 71, 72
leader election, 64
learners, 12
lexicographical ordering, 30
linear program, 19
linearizability, 82
Liskov, Barbara, 59
liveness, 10, 12, 25, 31, 53, 59
load, 3, 18, 23, 55, 68, 79, 110, 113
  induced by a strategy, 19
  lower bound, 19, 55, 68, 76, 87, 111
  system load, 19
load balancing, 2
Lynch, Nancy, 36

Maclaurin series, 115
majority, 1, 47
  ordinary, 1
  two-third, 1
Malkhi, Dahlia, 56, 72, 77
message delay, 9
message-passing, 6, 25
mutual exclusion, 2, 23

node vulnerability, 22
non-availability, 22

obstruction-free consensus emulation
  FastSynodOFC, 92–98
  SynodOFC, 32–36, 59, 60, 65, 91, 94, 96
operation, 6

concurrency, 10
pending, 10
precedence, 10
synchronous, 10, 88, 98, 102, 104, 105, 107
uncontended, 10, 74, 84, 88, 98, 102, 104, 105, 107

operation execution, 6
complete, 6
pending, 6

partition, 109
partition tolerance, 109
process, 5
available, 7
benign, 6
correct, 6
faulty, 6
propagation delay, 9
proposers, 12

quorum, 1, 15
δ-high quality, 111, 112
available, 25
cardinality, 22
Class-1, 83, 99, 105
Class-2, 83, 99, 105
Class-3, 83, 99
classes, 82
configuration, 37
hierarchy, 84
read, 26, 37
write, 26, 37
quorum reconfiguration, 36–38, 49
garbage collection, 36, 37, 45
quorum system, 15
t-resilient, 22
B-Grid, 18, 23
classical, 15, 32
CWalls, 23
dissemination, 83, 87
emulation based on a, 25
Fano plane, 17
FPP, 17, 23
Grid, 17, 23
optimally resilient, 22
Paths, 23
Singleton, 16, 23
Triangle Lattice, 23
two-thirds majority, 56
quorum systems, 1
ϵ-intersecting, 110–113
t-dissemination, 54–56, 76
t-masking, 68, 76
t-opaque, 76
(b,ϵ)-dissemination, 113–115
asymmetric read/write, 16, 26
Byzantine, 51, 52, 110
classical, 82, 109, 111, 113
dissemination, 52–56, 59, 65, 67, 68, 77, 79, 82, 102, 113
latency-efficient, 29, 81
masking, 52, 67–72, 74, 77, 82
non-blocking, 80
opaque, 52, 74–77
optimally resilient, 88
probabilistic, 109, 110
probabilistic dynamic, 116
probabilistic opaque, 115
refined, 82–91, 96, 98, 102, 107
signed, 116
strict, 109–111, 113
timed, 116
uniform t-refined, 87
uniform refined, 83

read inversion, 11
Reiter, Michael K., 56, 72, 77

replication, 1, 2, 31, 79, 81
Fast Paxos protocol, 82, 85, 91
Paxos protocol, 25, 31, 47, 81, 91
PBFT protocol, 59
resilience, 21–23, 54, 68, 109, 111, 112
ϵ-intersecting, 112, 113
optimal, 81
to a set system, 22

safety, 10, 12, 25, 59, 96
scheduler, 116
self-implementations, 77
set system, 15, 51, 82, 110
shared memory, 77
shared object, 6
shared-memory, 6
Shvartsman, Alex, 36
state machine, 5
step, 5
storage, 1–3, 9, 25
atomic, 25, 79, 82, 88, 91, 98, 110
atomicity, 10, 11, 26, 28, 29, 37, 98, 102, 110
multi-writer, 28
multi-writer multi-reader, 26, 52, 56, 79, 110
regular, 79, 82, 105, 110
regularity, 10, 11, 29, 110
safe, 68, 72, 77, 82
safeness, 10, 11, 71, 72, 74, 77, 85
single-round, 68, 69, 72, 81, 82, 107
single-writer, 11, 28, 72
single-writer multi-reader, 68, 72, 77, 79, 82, 88, 91, 98, 110
single-writer single-reader, 53, 69
storage emulation
ABD, 25–33, 36, 37, 40, 42, 47, 56, 58, 72, 74, 81, 99, 110
GV, 82, 91, 98–107
JCT, 77
MR, 68, 72–74, 77, 82, 85
MR2, 77
Phalanx, 52, 56–59, 72, 74, 79, 114
RAMBO, 5, 25, 36–47, 49
strategy, 15, 18, 19, 55, 110, 111
uniform access, 68, 113
synchronous model, 8

time-complexity, 9
timestamp, 2, 26, 33, 72, 75, 77
synchronization, 28
total order, 33
Toueg, Sam, 77

view, 59
changes, 64
Voronoi diagram, 49
voting, 1
weighted, 2
Vukolić, Marko, 98

wait-freedom, 10, 26, 28, 56, 98

Printed in the United States
by Baker & Taylor Publisher Services